D1342850

PLANTS FOR PROFIT

PLANTS FOR PROFIT

DOZENS OF WAYS
TO MAKE GARDENING PAY

BARTY PHILLIPS

PIATKUS

Acknowledgements

My thanks to John Phillips who did much of the research and thanks also to Rosamund Downs, Josephine Simons, Jean Clark, Marga and Guy Gervis and Hetty Gervis.

First published in 1990 by
Judy Piatkus (Publishers) Limited
5 Windmill Street, London W1P 1HF

British Library Cataloguing in Publication Data

Phillips, Barty
  Plants for profit
  1. Gardening
  I. Title
  635

  ISBN 0–86188–839–1

Design and illustrations by Zena Flax

Typeset in 11/12pt Linotron Sabon by
Phoenix Photosetting, Chatham, Kent
Printed in Great Britain by
Mackays of Chatham PLC, Chatham, Kent

Contents

Introduction

This book tells you how you can make money out of gardening – or the results of gardening. It is not offering fortunes, though there are people who make very good livings out of their garden. But if you are knowledgeable and confident you can certainly make a little money, and if you are single minded, energetic and entrepreneurial you could become a successful business.

If you are already growing vegetables for your family, say, and are producing more than you can eat, you can probably find a profitable outlet for the surplus. The recent publicity on the dangers of processed and chemically grown foods has alerted many people to the benefits of home grown, organic fruit and vegetables and this has opened up new possibilities for marketing such produce. If you are retiring or have children at school you may find you have time to make more of an existing hobby. You could extend your gardening interests to include gardening for other people or taking up a related craft such as drying or pressing flowers. Many a successful business has sprung from arranging flowers for a friend's wedding or selling a few pots of herbs at the garden gate.

Once a little confidence has been acquired there are many ways of selling, from local shops to craft markets, or even from your own home. There are, as you will discover, a surprising number of possible outlets for vegetables, plants or related objects or services.

This is not a gardening manual, but an ideas book, giving tips and advice for turning gardening into a profitable hobby or small business. These suggestions should be used alongside your existing gardening knowledge or reference books, and there is a list of further reading on page 173.

The chances of making money are quite good, provided that what you are offering is good quality, reasonably priced and well presented – and you find the right place to sell it. This book offers ideas for people who would like to make a full-time business out of their plants or who would just like to work part time when it suits them. There are ideas for people with large or small gardens and for people with no garden at all. But, part time or full time, you will only be successful if you proceed in a businesslike way. It may also be necessary for you to acquire extra skills.

The money-making schemes in this book are all based on personal experiences. They cover many aspects of the plant world, from growing vegetables and flowers to making objects such as pressed flower pictures, and edibles such as fruit preserves and herb vinegars. I hope that some of the ideas will spark off yet others, because if you have an interest and a skill, there's no reason why other people should not enjoy the results too.

The important thing is to find people who will buy your products before you plunge in too deep. It is better to grow because you enjoy it and begin gradually by selling to friends rather than by growing enormous quantities of something you then find you cannot sell.

Unless you have a professional training or have had experience in running a business, start slowly. Acquire an expertise in a particular form of growing, whether it be Chinese vegetables or fuchsias. If you enjoy flower arranging, learn how to become adept at arranging flowers for weddings or christenings. Try your skills out on friends and neighbours, then make enquiries locally. If there seems to be an interest in what you do, take it from there.

If you are eligible for a grant or need to raise money from the bank, make sure you have thoroughly researched your market and devised a business plan that works before you accept any offer of financial help. Make sure you start the scheme at the right time of year. It's no good starting a scheme which involves growing plants when it's too late to sow or propagate for that year. Grant schemes usually only last for a limited period so it is essential to make the most of that time and not waste it in an unproductive season. Ideally, prepare your detailed business plan, dig your land and assess your market over the winter, and arrange for the money to coincide with the start of the growing season when the work begins in earnest.

As for the time involved, you will be sure to find that your project takes up more of it than you ever imagined. People who cut a few flowers and put bunches of them at the garden gate with a box for the money will probably have the most opportunity for leisure, since they are simply supplying what they feel like and not reacting to demand. The moment you start selling through fairs, shops or to individual clients you will be fulfilling orders and kept very busy, even if only in spurts (as in the weeks before a craft fair or before Christmas).

What to ask yourself

There are many questions you should be asking yourself before you decide which way to go, for instance:

How much time do you have available?

Can you get financial backing?

Do you want a profitable hobby or a full-time job?

Are you prepared to get some extra training?

Is your forte food or flowers?

Do you have a sunny garden?

Do you have enough land to sustain a full-time business?

Would you consider digging up your lawn or flower beds to increase your growing area?

Are you prepared to work outdoors in all weathers?

Are you good at propagating?

Have you a greenhouse, or room for a greenhouse?

Are you aware of 'green' issues?

Do you have good/reliable/cheap suppliers locally who offer discounts?

Do you live near an inexpensive source of organic manure?

Are you artistic?

Do you enjoy craftwork?

Do you make your own jams and preserves?

Do you have space for storing equipment and finished items?

Are you prepared to keep abreast of the book keeping and business practice?

Will your family co-operate?

Do you enjoy working alone?

Would you mind working for other people?

Would you consider working in a partnership?

Are you gregarious?

Do you belong to any relevant clubs or societies?

Do you visit craft fairs?

Do you enjoy selling?

Do you have contacts with local newspapers?

Have you asked whether local shops or restaurants will take your produce?

Do you have suitable transport for equipment or produce?

Deciding on a project

The types of project you might consider fall into four main categories: food crops, flowers and foliage, gardening services, and 'offshoots', which include things made with plants such as pictures and preserves.

Food crops

This may sound like an easy option. You grow wonderful fresh green lettuces and your apple crop is far more than you can eat, so it sounds an obvious winner. But unfortunately everybody else's lettuces and apples are ripening at the same time, and the shops are full of fresh vegetables and fruit just when yours are at their peak. It is difficult to compete with large growers so you must be able to offer something fresher, healthier (i.e. organic) and more unusual.

This is not specifically an 'organic' book, but there is no doubt that organically grown vegetables and fruit have a marketing value that the small grower can exploit. If you sell vegetables that have been organically grown and freshly picked you are offering something special and highly desirable.

Unusual vegetables can also sell well in some areas of the country, but mainly where your customers are well-off and prepared to experiment in the kitchen. Before planting a large plot with anything out of the ordinary, do check that there is no immediate competition and that somebody will be prepared to buy your crop.

I've also included a section on growing herbs, which you can either sell locally or by mail order. Interest in different types of herbs is increasing.

Flowers and foliage

The decorative garden features quite largely in this book. Many people are now growing slightly unusual plants which are not readily available in garden centres. At the simplest level you can propagate plants from cuttings or seeds and sell them at local fairs or plant stalls. Or you can be more ambitious and prosper by running a specialist mail order plant business.

Gardening services

You don't need a garden yourself to offer gardening services to others. Many garden owners are actually incapable of looking after the garden themselves because they are too busy, too frail or just inexperienced. Such people are often glad of the services offered by professional or experienced gardeners. They may want someone to take over the entire responsibility of planning and planting the garden, or they may just require someone to tend one part of it.

Offshoots

Projects here include flower arranging, drying and pressing flowers and homemade jams and preserves – none of which require you to have a particularly large garden, just enthusiasm and a talent for your chosen craft.

Another idea is to serve teas in your garden. This can be profitable in its own right, but is also a way of attracting people into your garden who may then buy plants or produce.

There is a lot of interest in pretty products made out of flowers and plants. Look how prolifically dried flower arrangements and attractively packaged jams sell in the shops of The National Trust and stately homes open to the public. There are lots of possibilities here, but you must compete in quality, design and price with others doing a similar thing.

Please read the last chapter particularly carefully. It will tell you how to get professional advice of all kinds, which you will certainly need if you are going into business seriously. It will suggest the sort of questions you should be asking and anticipate the problems you may have to face. It will suggest how to get financial help, how to plan ahead, where to sell and market your product, how to tackle finances and legal requirements.

1
FOOD
CROPS

Organic
guidelines

Recent scares about the health content of our food have led to a huge increase in sales of organically grown fresh fruit and vegetables. Most major supermarket chains now sell organically grown food, and people will travel some distance to buy produce they know has been grown without chemical fertilisers, herbicides or pesticides. Freshness is important but we are all becoming aware that fresh fruit and vegetables don't in themselves constitute 'healthy' food – it's the method of production that counts.

There is a real demand for organic produce and this is an area where the 'beginner' can do well. Organic growing is hard work – no time-saving chemicals and pesticides are allowed and there is a lot of bending and lifting involved so you need a strong back – but it can be very rewarding and satisfying. This section discusses the basic principles of organic growing – from testing and feeding the soil to protecting your crops. The following section, beginning on page 26, deals with the more practical issues of what to grow.

The Soil Association If you want to advertise your produce as 'organically grown' you have to become a member of the Soil Association. This is a member of the International Federation of Organic Movements with similar organisations all over the world, and its aim is to promote the organic growing of food crops. Growing organically means feeding the soil with natural material and allowing the plants to draw on these as they need them, rather than using artificial fertilisers which allow the soil organisms to die out, the soil structure to break down and the soil itself to become unproductive in the long term.

Members of the Soil Association can have their soil tested and once it is approved they may carry the Soil Association symbol on their produce.

The Soil Association says that 'In general organic growing consists of sound rotations, the extensive and rational use of manure and vegetable wastes, the use of appropriate cultivation techniques, the avoidance of fertilisers in the form of soluble mineral salts and the prohibition of agrochemical pesticides. These all aid in the development of biological cycles involving micro-organisms, soil fauna, plants and animals which form the basis of organic agriculture.'

You don't have to have a large estate in the country to be able to grow vegetables organically. Town gardens can be adapted very successfully. But you must check your soil before you start as there have been instances where allotments were closed down because of unacceptable amounts of lead in the soil.

Starting off

First test your soil. If the Soil Association approve your soil, then you can start growing your vegetables and fruit and selling them as 'organically grown'.

However, it could take several years before your soil is acceptable to the Soil Association, and in the meantime you should follow the organic principles but sell your produce as non-organic.

When you have decided what vegetables you want to grow, group them into types (brassicas, legumes etc) and grow them in rotation (see below) or add the nourishment they require (see page 19).

Even in a small garden, where your vegetable beds are scattered among the flowers and shrubs, you can grow vegetables in rotation. The basic aims are the same: to fulfil the manurial needs of each vegetable and help it to resist pests and diseases.

Rotation of crops

Different vegetables have different soil and mineral requirements and can be categorised into three main groups:

Legumes (peas and beans) plus sweetcorn, spinach, chicory, endive, globe artichokes, onions, leeks and garlic.

Brassicas (cabbages, Brussels sprouts, broccoli, cauliflower, etc) plus swedes, turnips, kohl rabi.

Roots (carrots, parsnips, beetroot, salsify, celeriac, etc) plus marrows, melons, cucumbers, aubergines.

A rotation cycle ensures that the soil is nourished in a natural way. Normally three year rotation is used, with the land divided into four parts. One plot is used for permanent crops such as globe artichokes, asparagus, seakale, herbs and soft fruit. Each of the other three parts is devoted for one year to one of the three main groups above. After a year the brassicas are moved to the beds where the legumes were growing, the legumes are moved to where the roots were and the roots are put in the old brassica beds. The next year the vegetables change plots again, and in the fourth year they have returned to their original bed.

three-year rotation
legumes: add manure or compost
roots: add fertilizer
brassicas: add fertilizer and lime

1st year — legumes / roots / Permanent / brassicas

2nd year — brassicas / legumes / Permanent / roots

3rd year — roots / brassicas / Permanent / legumes

four-year rotation — legumes / roots / brassicas / green crop

Four-year rotations are now being used more frequently and may include a year when one bed is put down to a 'green crop' (see page 16) which is grown and dug back into the soil or has animals grazing on it. Alternatively, you can follow the brassica crop with a miscellaneous one which might include tomatoes, marrows, courgettes or melons.

Rotation of crops allows the mineral balance of the soil to be maintained and makes best use of organic matter. It also helps to keep plants healthy, as some pests and diseases which are attracted to one crop will not feed on another and are therefore not perpetuated in one place.

Fruits
Fruits do not rotate. Hard fruit such as apples and pears require an orchard, but soft fruits do not take up so much space and will crop the year after they have been planted.

Testing the soil

Most plants grow well in ordinary garden soil, but some will need special nourishment and conditions. Whether you are intending to grow organically or not you should test the ground to see whether it is acid or alkaline, and whether it needs any special attention. Clay soil – which retains water and lacks air – will need to be broken down and aerated with compost and peat, for example, in order for plants to grow successfully.

The pH scale is a means of measuring the acid/alkaline balance of the soil. Most garden soils vary between pH 6.0 (slightly acid) and pH 7.0 (neutral). An acid soil is one in which the pH content is below 7.0 and may be peaty, sandy and light or clayey and heavy. An acid soil has a low lime content while soils with a high lime content are alkaline.

A fairly simple soil testing kit can be obtained from chemists and horticultural sundriesmen. Some chemists offer a soil testing service. If you are a member of the Soil Association or Organic Farmers and Growers Ltd., you can have your soil tested by one of their inspectors. It is best to take samples from several different parts of the growing area. Keep the samples separate and keep a record of where each sample came from. Dig to a depth of 25cm (10in) for each sample.

Soils which have not been cultivated for many years may be very deficient in some of the elements needed for healthy growth. There are kits on the market for testing soils for nitrogen, phosphorus and potassium.

Treating deficiencies

Use organic rather than chemical fertilisers to treat your soil if you discover that your soil is deficient in any of the elements required by your crops.

Nitrogen deficiency (old leaves become yellow, young ones 'soft' and very green, plants stunted). Apply high nitrogen fertiliser such as dried blood.

Phosphorus deficiency (distinct blue leaves and stunted growth). Apply bone-meal fertilisers.

Potassium deficiency (small flowers and fruit, stunted plants, bronzing of leaves). Apply rock potash.

Magnesium deficiency (yellowing of leaves starting at veins). Apply seaweed meal or liquid animal manure.

Calcium deficiency (blossom-end rot in tomatoes, tip burn on lettuce, black-heart in celery, browned centres of Brussels sprouts). Incorporate plenty of manure or compost.

Sulphur deficiency (yellowing of leaves and stunted growth). Apply light dusting of calcium sulphate (horticultural gypsum).

Conditioning the soil The soil you use for growing is all important and the element which distinguishes a dead soil from a live one is humus. Humus is the complicated substance that gives the soil its true fertility. It is present in the soil as minute, black particles or as a jelly-like coating of the sand, silt and clay particles. Clay soils, particularly, need massive additions of humus in the form of farmyard manure, compost or peat, to break them down and introduce air.

Apart from changing the texture and structure of a soil, humus provides food for bacteria and fungi, and the conditions in which they can work.

Ways of keeping a good humus content

- Introduce plenty of well-rotted farmyard manure. Manure from neighbouring farms may *not* be organically acceptable depending on what the livestock are fed on. You should get this checked by the Soil Association.

- Practise green manuring as part of a four year rotation, if you can spare the space. Green manure is a crop grown and then dug back into the soil to add nutrients. Nitrogen cannot be used by many plants except in the form of a compound with at least one other element. Some green crops have nodules on their roots containing bacteria which help fix the nitrogen, and these crops should be dug into the soil while still young and green. Useful green manure crops which will fix nitrogen include Lucerne (*Medicago sativa*), Broad bean (*Vicia faba*), Red Clover (*Trifolium pratense*), Lupin (*Lupinus augustifolius*). Useful green manures which will not fix nitrogen include Mustard (*Sinapsis alba*), Phacelia (*Phacelia tanacetifolia*), Italian ryegrass (*Lolium multiflorum*).

- Mulching: a mulch is a thick layer of organic matter which helps to keep down weeds and retain moisture. Compost, spent mushroom compost, and peat also help to build up fertile top soil.

- Using a compost heap to make your own compost. Use all the vegetable waste from the garden and the kitchen (if you can be sure it has been organically raised). An enclosed system of composting is more efficient than an open heap which may cool down and dry out before the matter has fully decomposed (see page 18).
- Use soil conditioners such as calcium sulphate (horticultural gypsum) to create an open crumb structure on clay.
- Lime will also improve the texture of clay and peaty soils.

Soil aeration

It is crucial that the soil should hold air in order to allow the essential micro-organisms to breathe. In certain soils, particularly clay where drainage is bad, there will be too much water retention in the topsoil. Digging can be a help here.

Encourage worms which are instrumental in bringing air into the soil by boring, perforating and loosening the soil. Applying manure and compost helps to increase the worm population.

A worm box

Do not underestimate the importance of worms in the soil. They feed on organic matter and their waste is ejected as pellets which are coated in a gel. These pellets improve soil drainage and aeration and provide nutrients in a slow-release form which is easily assimilated by the plants. They also accelerate the decomposing process and produce good growing compost more quickly.

You can introduce worms into your garden by building a worm box. The brandling or tiger worm (*Eisenia foetida*), commonly used as fishermen's bait, is the one to use. It can be bought from fishing tackle shops or speciality suppliers.

The worms will eat their way through a variety of organic wastes, working from the bottom up. A well

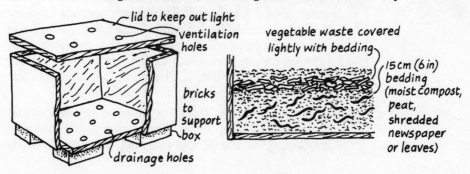

lid to keep out light
ventilation holes
bricks to support box
drainage holes

vegetable waste covered lightly with bedding
15 cm (6 in) bedding (moist compost, peat, shredded newspaper or leaves)

designed box will enable you to take the bottom layer of compost when it is ready and leave the worms to munch through the upper layers. The worm box should be kept at a temperature of around 20–24°C (68–75°F). Water the material if it looks as though it's getting dry.

The worm compost is rather rich and indigestible to plants, so use it sparingly. Scatter between vegetable rows and sprinkle on to the seed bed before sowing.

The compost heap

An enclosed heap works better than an open one because it will remain warmer and encourage decomposition. In a well-made heap, rubbish should be compost within three months in warm weather or up to six in cold weather.

There are various composting bins available on the market but it is more satisfactory to make your own from wooden planks. A capacity of about 0.5 cu m (15 cu ft) is suitable for a small garden with limited vegetable waste. Two heaps are better than one because you can be filling up the second while the first is decomposing.

Build up the heap with 15 to 20cm (6 to 8in) layers of vegetable waste. If you are short of material, buy straw, wet it thoroughly and incorporate it. Spread farmyard manure or sulphate of ammonia at 15g to 1sq m (½oz to 1sq yd) over alternate layers and a sprinkling of lime over intervening layers or use a proprietary activator over each layer.

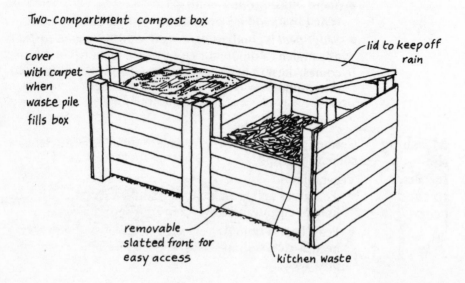

Two-compartment compost box

cover with carpet when waste pile fills box

lid to keep off rain

removable slatted front for easy access

kitchen waste

Water the heap as you build it up. When it is full, cover it with 2.5cm (1in) of soil.

If the heap goes cold or dry before it has finished decomposing, turn it with a fork so the top of the heap ends up in the middle. Water it as you turn it.

Feeding the soil

The best sources of manure for feeding and enriching the soil are plenty of well-rotted farmyard manure from all types of livestock and vegetable wastes which have been composted. Avoid inorganic fertilisers with chemicals which promise to act fast and give miraculous results – they are soon washed out of the soil and damage some of the micro-organisms in the finely tuned natural eco-system. The Soil Association does allow for certain difficulties which face even the most conscientious organic farmer and may suggest a small amount of certain nitrates for a limited period where growth is particularly poor.

Use proprietary organic fertilisers when necessary:

- Mixtures of animal wastes such as *blood, fish and bone meal* contain high percentages of nitrogen and promote good root growth.
- *Hoof and horn fertiliser* releases nitrogen into the soil slowly and steadily which is very handy when manure supplies are short.
- *Seaweed fertilisers* make good soil conditioners and get bacterial action going.
- *Spent mushroom compost* can be used (it should be tested first) and is specially good for mulching.
- *Sedge peat* is good for improving a soil's texture. Apply it as a mulch to suppress weed growth, then, when the time comes, dig it in before sowing and it will be broken down into humus.

Matching the fertiliser to the crop

Certain plants need *extra* feeding to do their best. Here are some useful tips.

Vegetables
- Tomatoes and green peppers should have a potash fertiliser to encourage flower and fruit formation.
- Peas, beans, onions, leeks, celery, spinach and tomatoes need a rich soil and as much manure and compost as possible.

- Peas and beans can 'fix' nitrogen from the air to enrich the soil (see also 'green manures', page 16).
- Brassicas are grown after legumes in the rotation because they need a lot of nitrogen. Supplement the nitrogen left by the legumes with a general fertiliser of nitrogen (N), phosphoric acid (P_2O_5) and potash (K_2O) in equal quantities.
- The brassica plot is generally given an application of lime to prevent club root.
- Root vegetables should receive only a general fertiliser, no manure. And no lime, since there will be enough left over from the previous year's brassicas.
- Potatoes grown alongside the roots can be manured but should have no lime because it may encourage scab.

Fruit
- All soft fruit should be given blood, fish and bone meal in a wide circle round the plant, to reach the root tips. A mulch of compost round the stem will supply all trace elements.
- Red and white currants and gooseberries require a lot of potassium. Apply potash to the soil.
- Blackcurrants need a lot of nitrogen; feed with hoof and horn meal.
- Raspberries should be mulched with well-rotted manure in late winter. Apply seaweed to counteract iron deficiency.
- Blueberries require an acid soil.

To sum up
Peas, beans, onions, leeks, shallots, lettuces, endive, celery and radish may be given lots of manure and compost.

Cabbages, Brussels sprouts, savoys, cauliflower, broccoli, kale and spinach should be given general fertilisers and lime (if a soil test indicates the need).

Beetroot, carrots, turnips, swedes, parsnips, celeriac, salsify, scorzonera and chicory should be given general fertiliser only.

Soft fruit should be given blood, fish and bone meal and garden compost.

Fruit trees should be planted in deep soil with plenty of compost and good drainage. If the soil is very acid, use a little lime. Fruits with stones rather than pips like plenty of lime, whereas apples prefer less.

Protecting vegetables

Cloches

In warm climates if the soil temperature is high enough, spinach, carrots, peas, broad beans, spring onions and potatoes can be sown direct into the soil in late winter.

In cooler climates it is possible to grow many crops about a month earlier than usual if they are protected by cloches. These include early broad beans, early cabbage, cauliflowers, early peas, spinach, early turnips and beetroot.

For early crops the cloches should be put in place about three weeks before they are required in order to let the soil warm up before planting out. After protecting an early crop, the cloches can be used to cover tender vegetables such as tomatoes, peppers or courgettes. Make sure the ground is wet when you set up the cloches as they will then help to conserve the moisture.

Lift the cloches by degrees, to allow the plants to harden off gently. To begin with, open the ends during the day and cover them again at night.

In midsummer another sowing of the 'early' vegetable crops can be made and the cloches can be used, greenhouse fashion, to mature them in early autumn. They can also be used to ripen tomatoes, which may still be green in early autumn.

Cloches used inside a greenhouse during cold weather will keep delicate crops alive without the need to heat the greenhouse.

Cloches also protect crops from heavy rain and birds.

There are two basic types of cloche available, glass or plastic, though they come in various forms. Glass is good but expensive and liable to break. Plastic is easily stored and the sheeting can be renewed each year. Rigid cloches come in different shapes and sizes. Choose those which are wide enough and tall enough to give room for the plants to grow, and make sure they can be pinned or weighted to the ground or they may blow away. Tunnel cloches are a cheap way of

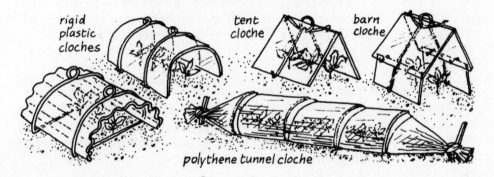

rigid plastic cloches

tent cloche

barn cloche

polythene tunnel cloche

protecting a lot of vegetables. They are constructed of wire hoops and plastic sheeting and must be securely fixed. They can be very long or divided into sections.

black polythene sheeting

bury edges of sheeting firmly in soil

Black polythene sheeting

Use black polythene sheeting when you grow potatoes, tomatoes, peas, beans, etc. It is especially good if you want to start sowing early. It protects the seeds from birds, helps keep the ground warm, stops weeds growing and helps retain moisture.

Anchor the sheeting down on the surface of the bed after sowing seeds. Once the seeds come up, make a slit in the sheeting and let the plant grow through. Leave the sheeting in place until you harvest or need to water.

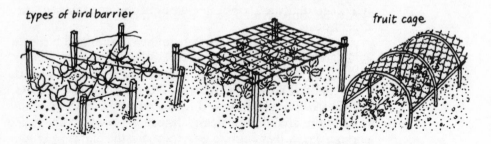

types of bird barrier

fruit cage

Bird barrier

Some vegetable crops such as peas and new young shoots of lettuces are eaten by birds. Pieces of thread tied to sticks and zig zagging over the rows make an effective bird barrier.

Protecting fruit

- Protect less hardy fruit blossoms (peaches, nectarines and apricots, etc) from frost with fine netting. Protect cherries and raspberries from birds in the same way.
- Fig shoots should be protected from frost by wrapping the plant up in straw and hessian.

- Currants and gooseberries should be protected from severe frost when in flower by covering the bushes with fine netting. This will also protect the fruit later on.
- Wasps may be seduced away from fruit by a jampot half full of beer or cider covered in paper with a small hole in it. Once in the jar the wasps are trapped.
- To avoid red spider mite on fruit, spray with water (or derris, see page 25).
- A well-built fruit cage covered in netting is the best protection against birds.
- Strawberries can be protected from frost with loose straw and from frost and birds with cloches (see pages 21–2).

The healthy garden

It is important to create a healthy growing environment as the healthier and stronger your plants, the more resistant they will be to disease and the better able to throw off any sickness. In addition the garden itself will not encourage pests and diseases.

- Always buy healthy plants.
- Always burn plants with any sign of disease. Never put them on the compost heap.
- Always burn fruit tree prunings in case they harbour disease.
- Don't put potatoes on the compost heap which might become contaminated by potato blight.
- Use only pots and seed trays that have been sterilized with boiling water.
- Keep the greenhouse clean (see below).
- Keep a look out for the first signs of pests and fungus. If you see a caterpillar, pick it off and drown it in water. Rub off greenfly with finger and thumb. Pick off any mildewed leaves and throw them away.
- Constant vigilance is very important to keep weeds at bay. Regular hoeing will prevent persistent weeds from flourishing and, above all, prevent them from seeding.
- Put healthy annual weeds straight on the compost heap.

Cleaning out a greenhouse

To prevent pests and diseases in the greenhouse, you should make sure it is kept scrupulously clean and tidy all through the year. Do not keep dirty trays, boxes and pots in it or leave plant or other rubbish lying around. Cracked and broken panes let in rain and let out heat and should be replaced as soon as possible. If the glass is very dirty it may keep out up to 40 per cent of daylight, especially through the roof. It is easier to prevent dirt building up on the glass than to clean it off, and regular hosing down of the exterior is a good idea. The interior should be washed with soapy water at least once a year.

Friends and neighbours

An organic system should aim towards letting the pests take care of themselves – or rather encouraging beneficial insects and animals to feed off the pests. You can help in this process as some plants seem to attract certain pest predators.

- Pot marigolds (*Calendula*) and African and French marigolds (*Tagetes*), poppies (*Papaver*), nasturtiums (*Tropaeolum*) and *Convolvulus tricolor* definitely attract hover flies which eat aphids, so should be grown next to crops which are susceptible, such as broad beans. Lace wings also eat aphids and they are attracted to the garden by a variety of plants in close proximity.

- Hedgehogs are excellent predators. Encourage them with cat or dog food, not bread and milk which are bad for them. You can provide them with a wooden box in which to hibernate during winter – put hay in the bottom to keep them warm.

- Bats are excellent insect eaters (and a protected species). You can get bat boxes to encourage them to nest. Pipistrelles are the most common. They swoop about with the swallows at dusk catching insects.

- Toads and frogs eat insects and slugs. A small pond will attract both birds and frogs. Make one out of a wooden barrel (from garden centres). Keep filling the barrel until the wood swells and becomes watertight. Sink it into a hole and make sure it is level. If you fill a large plastic box with earth or a piece of turf and put it in the barrel, this will allow frogs to climb out.

- Birds, though they eat fruit, will also protect it. They eat slugs, grubs, caterpillars and aphids. Encourage them by introducing bird tables, baths and nesting boxes.

- *Bacillus thuringiensis* is a parasitic bacterium that attacks the digestive system of some caterpillars and can be beneficial to outdoor crops.

Organic pesticides and fungicides

As a last resort you may have to turn to organic pesticides and fungicides to protect your crops. These are comparatively safe and remain active only for a day or so, and won't harm humans or animals, but they should always be used with care.

Insecticidal soap, quassia, derris, pyrethrum, rotenone, nicotine, copper fungicide and dispersive sulphur are all permitted by the Soil Association.

In general, if you can get away without using them do so, but if a plant has a fungus disease that still persists after the affected part has been removed and burned, an organic fungicide is the only answer.

Organic fruit
and vegetables

Many of the people I interviewed for this book are organic growers and find it a very satisfactory and rewarding way of life. Supermarket chains are beginning to offer organic fruit and vegetables but the produce is often fairly expensive and in some shops far from fresh. So there's plenty of scope for selling freshly picked, well presented produce.

Today the market for organic produce is divided between growers who turn over 90 per cent of their stock to the distributor (in return for guaranteed sales) and those who choose to remain independent and distribute the goods themselves.

There are good reasons for remaining independent: major supermarket chains are fussy about the presentation of their goods, selecting only shiny, unblemished, uniformly sized and perfectly formed items. This is a real problem when it comes to organic fruit because these qualities are often artificially produced. Also, once a grower has signed his or her entire stock over, there is no good organic produce to offer to a local market.

Organic gardening is much more labour intensive than chemically assisted growing, as you will have seen from the previous chapter. If you already grow vegetables you could use your know-how and expand your operation, selling the surplus to make a profit. One fit person with plenty of enthusiasm and time to give to the enterprise could probably cultivate up to 6,000sq m (1½ acres). If you work a larger plot of land you will need some assistance. The examples I include in this section follow the growing of one comparatively large garden and one small farm.

It is perfectly possible to grow quite a large amount of produce in a smaller area for the family and simply sell the surplus if and when you happen to have any. The average allotment-sized area or fairly small back garden or vegetable plot can produce a surprising amount of food crops if planned wisely. (Council allotment holders are not officially allowed to sell their produce.)

Vegetable gardening in small spaces

There are several ways of using a limited area to the full. You can, for example, sow vegetables closer together in the rows, especially if you choose small but heavy cropping varieties. Intercropping, catch cropping, successional sowing and implementing the deep bed system are other options.

Inter-cropping

Intercropping is a space-saving method of sowing or planting which exploits the differences in growth rates between crops. Fast grown crops are sown between slow maturers. By the time the slow growers are big enough to fill all the space, the fast growing ones will have been harvested.

Spring onions, short-rooted carrots, small beetroot, radishes, kohl rabi and spinach all make good fast growing fill-ins with slower maturing brassicas.

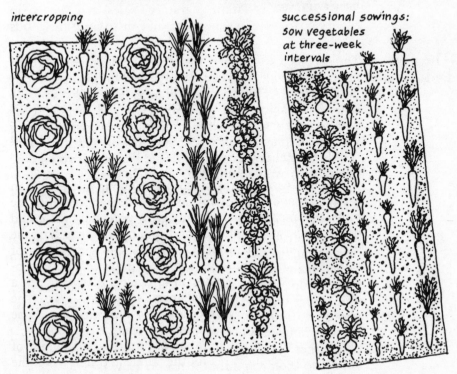

intercropping

successional sowings: sow vegetables at three-week intervals

Catch cropping

Catch crops are crops which are grown comparatively quickly and can be sown between harvesting and sowing of slower growing vegetables, or sown at the same time and harvested quickly, leaving space for the slow growers to fill gradually.

Good salad crops and vegetables for catch cropping and intercropping in succession between slower growing brassicas would be: lettuces (*Lactuca sativa*) 9 weeks, American cress or land cress (*Barbarea praecox*) 9 weeks, corn salad or lamb's lettuce (*Valerianella locusta*) 12 weeks, radishes (*Raphanus sativus*) from 6 weeks, kohl rabi (*Brassica oleracea caulorapa*) and globe beetroot (*Beta vulgaris*) 8 weeks, endive (*Chicorum endivia*) 12 weeks plus 2 weeks for blanching, asparagus peas (*Lotus tetragonolobus*) 12 weeks, carrots (*Daucus carota*) 10 weeks, spinach (*Spinacia oleracea*) 11 weeks.

Successional sowings

Successional sowings (sowing the same vegetables at intervals to avoid a glut) also make good use of the space available. Be ready to fill any ground which becomes vacant unexpectedly (which may happen if a crop has failed or been harvested early).

The deep bed system

The deep bed system of growing vegetables involves growing them in wide beds of around 1.2m (4ft) instead of long narrow ones. This cuts out unnecessary paths and can double the amount of growing space and so practically double your crop, which is an important consideration if you are hoping to grow enough to sell. Narrow paths should be left between the beds for easy access as you should not actually walk on the bed. If you do have to stand on it for any reason, use a wide plank which will distribute your weight.

The system is not just deep in width, but in depth too. The idea being to dig deeply, incorporate a lot of bulky organic matter which encourages plants to grow down rather than spread out so they can be planted closer together. In heavy soils the beds may be raised so that they drain more easily. The seeds can be sown so that they are almost touching and should be planted in squares or oblongs rather than in rows. The seedlings are not thinned out, rather you begin harvesting when they are still very young, to leave room for the rest to grow large.

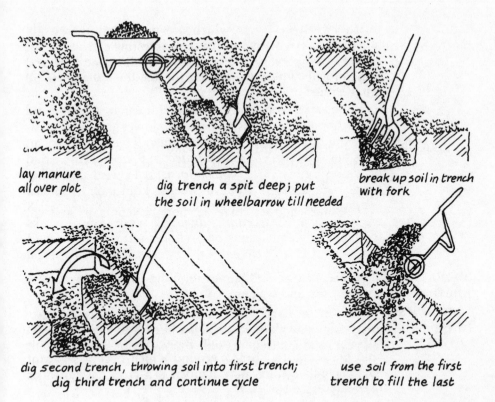

lay manure
all over plot

dig trench a spit deep; put
the soil in wheelbarrow till needed

break up soil in trench
with fork

dig second trench, throwing soil into first trench;
dig third trench and continue cycle

use soil from the first
trench to fill the last

Most vegetables are suitable for deep bed cultivation, in particular tomatoes, marrows, aubergines, brassicas and onions.

Extending the growing season

Some crops can stay in the ground and be harvested all winter. These include purple sprouting broccoli, Brussels sprouts, spring and winter cabbages, kale, turnips for their leaves, kohl rabi, leeks, autumn sown onions and spinach.

Winter cropping salads include celeriac, chicory, Chinese cabbage, corn salad, endive, American or land cress, lettuce under cloches, radish, salsify, Welsh onion and chop suey greens (a form of annual chrysanthemum).

What to grow

Different varieties of plants have better resistance to pests and diseases. Choose varieties of fruit, in particular, which are mildew resistant, because once established on a plant, mildew will move on to affect other varieties. Modern plants are bred for their resistance to disease so check on new varieties before deciding what to grow. F1 hybrids are first generation crosses between two selected parents and are particularly vigorous and this helps them to resist early attacks of disease. Varieties of potato vary greatly according to local conditions. Make sure that the tubers you buy are certified to be disease free.

Vegetables

The following types of organically grown vegetables are most likely to be accepted by large distributors: carrots, onions, leeks, potatoes, brassicas, beets, field beans, tomatoes and cucumbers (which give a particularly good return).

Personal shoppers may be more adventurous and you could probably sell them more unusual vegetables.

Some unusual vegetables to try

Planting, sowing and harvesting times will vary according to area, site and season.

American or Land Cress is a hardy, low-growing, fast-maturing salad plant which tastes like watercress. Available all year round, it requires soil with plenty of organic matter and likes damp, semi-shade. It is ready eight weeks after sowing. Sow from March to June for summer picking, July to September for winter and spring picking. Cover with bracken, straw or cloches during winter. Pick individual leaves as required. Ideal for small town gardens.

Aubergines need a warm climate or greenhouse cultivation. Water with liquid fertiliser every two weeks when in full growth. In temperate climates, start them off under cloches and keep them covered until they grow too tall for the cloches.

Celeriac is a bushy plant with celery-like leaves. The swollen base is a good substitute for celery but it is hardier and less vulnerable to disease. Celeriac needs an open site and well-drained soil and has a long growing season (six months from sowing to harvest). Give plenty of water and from June onwards, apply liquid manure weekly.

Chicory Some varieties are grown for forcing and the 'chicons' are dug up and blanched in deep, moist peat. They are popular as a winter vegetable and can fetch high prices. Others form heads for cooking or use in salads.

Chinese Mustard (*Pak Choi*) has thick, dark, glossy leaves with no heart. It needs a rich, moist soil but tolerates light shade. It is not frost hardy. Can be sown in succession during summer but may run to seed in dry weather. It will re-sprout if chopped at ground level. Ready nine weeks after sowing.

Garlic needs a rich, well dug soil and an open, sunny position. It must be watered in summer. Plant bulbs in late winter and spring for main winter crop and in late summer and autumn under cloches in the greenhouse for early harvesting the following year. Lift when the leaves die down in autumn. Dry in the sun or any warm place for two days. Hang in a cool airy place indoors.

Globe Artichokes can be grown as annuals or perennials on a sunny sheltered site. Cut heads while still closed. Harvest from summer to early autumn.

Hamburg Parsley is a very hardy form of parsley with edible foliage and roots. It will grow in semi-shade in moist, poorish soil. It is slow to germinate and has a long growing season. Mix with radish seeds to mark the rows until it appears. It can be left in soil all winter. Mulch with bracken or straw to make lifting easier in frosty weather.

Kohl Rabi have swollen stems and are cooked like turnip. Harvest from early summer.

Mangetout are also known as snap peas and snow peas. The pods and seeds are all eaten. Harvest from late spring to mid autumn.

Peppers (*Capsicum*) develop as bushy plants. In colder climates they do best under glass but can do surprisingly well out of doors in sheltered areas if started under cloches. Water with liquid fertiliser every two weeks when in full growth. If you want bright red or coloured fruits you must choose a suitable variety. 'Luteus' is a variety that starts green and turns yellow and 'Canape' will turn red when ripe.

Rhubarb Chard, a red version of Swiss chard (or Seakale Beet), makes a decorative plant in the vegetable or flower garden and is good to eat. The stalks are cooked like celery and the leaves like spinach. Germination time is 10 to 14 days and it can be harvested 12 weeks after sowing. Harvest mid summer.

Salsify and **Scorzonera** both have long roots which don't take up much garden space but they do have a long growing season. Grow for roots in winter and young shoots in spring. They need an open site, stone-free soil and *no* fresh manure (or the roots will split). Sow in April or May to harvest in October. Water in dry weather, and then mulch.

Summer Squashes are relations of the marrow and just as

easy to grow. Most have trailing growth. Some squashes are used while young and green like courgettes. Others are allowed to mature until their skins become hard. Harvest from mid summer.

Chinese vegetables

Even more unusual are Chinese vegetables which are becoming more familiar and more popular.

Chinese Cabbage Varieties:

Jade Pagoda (F1 hybrid), tall cylindrical heads.

Tip Top (F1 hybrid), bright green, barrel shape heads, compact and tightly packed. Good resistance to bolting.

Two Seasons (F1 hybrid), well packed hearts, said to be very resistant to bolting – can be sown in spring or summer.

Celery Mustard Varieties:

Baak-Choy (Chinese leaves), broad white midribs, deep green leaves. Can be used like celery.

Tsai Shim, grown for its flowering stems, picked rather like sprouting broccoli.

Other varieties:

Chinese Mustard, also known as 'Green in the Snow', very hardy winter vegetable with a spicy, slightly hot flavour and deep green leaves.

Edible Burdock or Watanabe Early, produces long slender roots with a nutty flavour.

Garland chrysanthemum, also known as chop suey greens or Shungiku. Deeply cut, strongly aromatic foliage.

Japanese Greens (*Mizuna*) or Tokyo Belle, dark green deeply cut leaves with a fresh, crisp taste. Hardy, can get an early spring crop from a late summer sowing.

Notes on cultivation: These vegetables like an open sunny position and a rich moisture-retentive soil. Many of these varieties have a tendency to run to seed if they receive any check to growth so all types should be sown direct where they are to grow. Sowing times vary.

Fruit

Apples are difficult to sell as they grow so well and there is always a glut. Unless you are going to turn them into apple jelly or pies, they are not a good business bet. There may be a greater demand for pears, plums and cherries. Special old-fashioned varieties are becoming very popular, however, and could be an area to specialise in. If you are planting trees specially you will have to wait a few years for them to mature.

Apples will keep and travel well, but soft fruit will only keep for a couple of days and should be carefully packed in small punnets to avoid squashing.

Soft fruit bushes and canes can crop well for at least ten years after they have been planted so, before planting clear the ground well of perennial weeds with creeping root systems (such as convolvulus, couch grass and ground elder), because it is difficult to clear such weeds from the shallow roots of fruit bushes. You will need fruit cages or nets to protect the fruit from birds.

Apples
- Plant in deep soil with good drainage. Dig in plenty of well-rotted manure or garden compost.
- Add a little lime to very acid soils.
- Don't allow grass to grow round the base of the tree for the first few years.
- Cropping is improved by cross pollination, so plant more than one variety. Choose varieties that flower at the same time, and that are compatible.
- 'Sunset' is similar to but easier to grow than 'Cox's Orange Pippin'. 'Lord Lambourne' is a regular and heavy cropper.
- Good cookers are 'Arthur Turner', 'Grenadier' and 'George Neal'.

Blackcurrants
- Feed the bed generously with manure and hoof and horn meal.
- Plant 1.2m (4ft) apart.
- Mulch with comfrey or garden compost covered with lawn mowings every second year.
- The bushes fruit on one- and two-year-old branches.
- 'Seabrook's Black' is mite and virus resistant.

Gooseberries
- Preparation and planting as for blackcurrants (above).
- Mulch with comfrey and lawn mowings or potash to supply potassium.
- Choose bushes with long stems between soil and branches so that you can weed under them.

- Prune branches to third or fourth outward pointing bud to prevent fruiting in first year and encourage roots and branches to put out growth. In future years, shorten branches by about a third and remove all central and small branches so that air and sunshine can get into the bush. This discourages mildew and helps to ripen the fruit.
- 'Langley Gage' and 'Whitesmith' are mildew resistant varieties.

Hybrid berries such as Tayberry, Loganberry, Boysenberry and Youngberry

- Prepare the ground with manure and bonemeal.
- Plant deep and train on wire supports. They don't mind a shady position.
- These berries have the advantage of ripening late, when raspberries are over. Harvest in late summer.

Pears

- Pear trees prefer heavy but well-drained soil.
- Plant in a protected site where frost won't damage the blossom.
- 'William's Bon Chrétien' is a good autumn variety, 'Doyenné du Comice' and 'Winter Nelis' both ripen in winter.

Plums and Cherries

- In mid spring feed with 20–35g nitro chalk or sulphate of ammonia per sq. metre (½–1oz per sq. yard) and similar amounts of sulphate of potash in late winter, plus 40g (1½oz) super phosphate every third autumn.
- 'Dennison's Superb' is a very fertile dessert plum.
- 'Quetsche' is a rich flavoured stewing plum that is self fertilising. 'Merryweather' is a heavy cropping damson.
- 'Merton' is a sweet cherry which cross pollinates with 'Bigarreau Napoleon'. Morello cherries are self fertile.

Raspberries

- Prepare the ground with manure and bonemeal and seaweed fertiliser.
- Plant young canes in November, shorten them to 30cm (1ft) and tie into the bottom of the support fence. Canes should be 30cm (1ft) apart, rows 1.2m (4ft) apart.
- Remove old canes in autumn and tie the new year's

growth into the support fence. New shoots will appear in spring.

- Weed the beds for the first year; in following years mulch with comfrey, manure or lawn mowings in May or June. Fork in the mulch in autumn.
- The following varieties provide a succession of fruit: 'Malling Promise' (early season), 'Malling Jewel' (mid season), 'Malling Admiral' (late season).

Strawberries

- Prepare the bed with plenty of manure or compost and coarse bonemeal and rake to a fine tilth.
- Plant in August or September, 30cm (1ft) apart in rows 60cm (2ft) apart.
- Hoe and mulch the bed in spring with peat or straw to protect the plants from slugs.
- Netting held in place by cut-off plastic containers filled with stones, will keep off the birds. Protect against the strawberry aphid by spraying with a nicotine and soap wash in April or May. Use pyrethrum in the evenings once the flowers appear.
- Remove the runners in autumn and start a new bed. Strawberries do not flourish when grown in the same place too long.
- Maincrop strawberries fruit in June and July, perpetual from June to October, alpines between June and the first frost. Disease-resistant varieties include 'Cambridge Rival' and 'Cambridge Late Prince' (maincrop), 'La Sans Rivalle' which is tolerant of light or chalky soils (perpetual), 'Alexandria' (alpine).

Rhubarb

- Rhubarb should crop well for about 15 years so it is worth preparing the bed with care. Dig in coarse bonemeal, manure or compost and a barrowload of natural mattress stuffing or feathers to each square metre.
- Plant the crowns in late autumn 70cm (2ft 4in) apart.
- Clear dead leaves in late autumn and mulch with bonemeal and 30cm (1ft) dead leaves covered with netting. Do not pick during the first year.
- Rhubarb can be forced after the third year by covering the plant with a bottomless bucket in late winter or early spring. Remove the bucket when the stems reach the top.

- Pick by pulling the stems off at the base. Stop picking at the beginning of August to allow the plants to gain strength for the following year.
- Trouble-free varieties include 'Hawke's Champagne' and 'Timperley Early'.

Fruit and vegetables on patios

Even if you have no garden but just a small courtyard, you can grow a good number of fruit and vegetables in growing bags and other containers, especially if you choose heavy cropping, small stature plants including green peppers, cucumbers and certain types of tomatoes. Small space-saving fruit trees are now available thanks to special rootstocks.

Hanging baskets and window boxes are specially useful for growing strawberries and herbs in. Strawberries can also be grown in strawberry barrels or pots, which can accommodate a large number of plants.

Organic grow bags are expensive, but can be made at home, using heavy-duty polythene bags which once had peat or fertiliser in them or heavy-duty polythene sheeting stapled together with heavy-duty staples. Fill them with suitable compost. Lie the bags longways, cut crosses in the top and plant through these.

Possible crops for sheltered patios

Grapes in pots (choose a suitable variety for the climate – they don't necessarily need very warm conditions), strawberries (in special barrels), melons, citrus fruits and courgettes. Peppers, aubergines, tomatoes and other slightly tender crops will benefit from the shelter of a wall. Cherry tomatoes can make a fine display grown in hanging baskets.

Possible crops for very small corners

Dwarf French beans (*Phaseolus vulgaris*), cherry tomatoes, baby-headed cabbages, beetroot (will tolerate partial shade), 'Tom Thumb' and 'Little Gem' lettuce (grow throughout the year in any little pot or container and in used grow bags), lamb's lettuce and radishes.

Possible crops for indoors

A surprisingly abundant amount of fruit and vegetables can be grown inside the house if you are prepared to use your home as an indoor garden. Provided the plants have adequate light and a suitable temperature there are plenty of small crops you can grow.

On windowsills and under rooflights you can grow cherry tomatoes, radishes, aubergines, peppers, mustard and cress, lettuces, strawberries, alfalfa sprouts, bean sprouts and herbs of all kinds. Grow in anything from old tea caddies to oil cans and chamber pots, chimney pots, lined baskets (use heavy-duty polythene for the lining), pots, pans, prams, old sinks – the possibilities for containers are endless.

Remember, however, that vegetables need a far greater intensity of light when grown indoors than ordinary room light. For poorly lit spaces there are 'growing' lights available under which plants will grow satisfactorily.

Preservation

Try to keep your produce looking fresh and crisp or juicy.

- Don't pick until the last minute.
- Wash off mud, but not obsessively which might bruise the items.
- Keep in a cool place (especially soft fruits) and under cover.
- Put vulnerable items (salad vegetables) in plastic bags.
- If turnover is slow put salads in salad section of refrigerator.
- Root crops should survive well if kept in the dark and cool.
- Herbs and green vegetables will last longer if their roots or stems are kept standing in water, which should be changed frequently.

IDEAS IN PRACTICE

A large garden

Christopher Parker owns a three acre strip of garden in which he has a small apple orchard. He has always grown vegetables for the family and for years he kept cows as well. In 1980, when he was 62, he realised that working his own land was what he really enjoyed most in life. He took early retirement from his job in agricultural research in order to continue his hobby on a slightly larger scale and, he hoped, make a little money out of it. He has been growing organic vegetables for sale on about one and a half acres ever since.

Growing and tending

Christopher Parker grows red and green cabbages, carrots, potatoes, sweetcorn, broccoli, spring and bulb onions, parsley, chives, leeks, lettuces, radishes, curly kale, courgettes, beetroot, rhubarb. All through winter, in succession, he grows chicory as a high paying main crop and radicchio, a reddish-leaved salad plant, and has a 55m (60yd) row of runner beans. He also grows 'Lots and lots of leeks which are terrific, the most profitable and the easiest vegetable to grow'.

Among the vegetables he grows grass and mustard for cultivation as green manure, marigolds, sweet peas and a host of mopheaded asters and outdoor chrysanthemums. There are also blue chicory flowers from the previous year's crop among the vegetables which are sold as cut flowers.

Christopher is a member of the Soil Association (see pages 12 and 172). All his produce is now Soil Association Approved under their 'symbol' scheme and he displays the symbol whenever he sells his vegetables. 'It's quite expensive to join this. Following their strict rules has cost me a good deal more.' He originally bought pig dung from a neighbour but when The Soil Association tested a sample they found it contained copper (which is used as a medicinal preventative) and would not let him use it if he wanted to use the 'symbol' label, so now he gets cow dung – which has been accepted.

'The land is very fertile because it was grazed by my cows for 30 years and I like digging, though in fact I never do any now. Twenty years ago I already had a bad back and thought I might not be able to dig, so I bought a small cultivator. For working on my larger area of vegetables I have now added another cultivator and two mowers and I occasionally hire a tractor from a neighbour.

'The main problem is weed control. I try to deal with it by, as far as possible, preventing weeds from seeding. That's the only way I can keep on top of them. I do it mainly with a wheel hoe, used repeatedly, together with some hand weeding and some weeding on hands and knees with a knife.' Weeding is a constant chore. No sooner has he finished one section than weeds crop up elsewhere so it's a Forth Bridge operation which he does whenever he has time.

Selling

On Tuesdays Christopher Parker takes some of his produce to the local natural food shop and every Saturday morning he sets up a stall in a back street in his local town, where a queue of loyal customers waits to buy. In summer he has flowers as well. 'The bunches are very small but the rich can buy several and the less well off can buy one.' By mid-day everything is sold and he is on his way home again.

It took some time to find a satisfactory way of selling his organic crops. The initial thinking was to ask customers to telephone orders in advance and then collect from his address. He advertised in the local papers but there was literally no response, 'so I realised there was no future in that. Then I heard about a little group of people selling bric a brac in an extreme back street in town so I joined them.' They were pushed around a bit by the local council and had to move several times to make way for new building developments but he now has planning permission to set up his stall outside a health food shop.

'Ninety per cent of my customers come every week. There's always a struggle at the beginning of the day because I transport everything in my ancient Volvo, unload the vegetables and the two folding tables, then remove the car from traffic warden reach. In summer when I get back at about 8.30 am there are sometimes people already waiting. I often do not get time to set up my notice or attach the prices all morning.

'Basically I get my kicks out of customer satisfaction. I think it's a socially useful thing to do. I wouldn't do it without the money mind you, but I do get satisfaction out of the fact that as far as I know I am the only person who is producing organic vegetables and selling them direct to the consumer on this kind of scale in this area.'

His living expenses are low and are covered by his state pension and a small industrial pension so the money he makes on his vegetables he can spend on what he likes. The garden does, however, take up all his time. 'I actually have very little leisure time. I spent my first profits on a stationary caravan on the coast where I do sea canoeing but this is the first year since retiring that I have been able to take a holiday. It would probably be more profitable and less hard work to grow a much more restricted range of crops (perhaps concentrating on leeks, tomatoes, peppers, cabbages and chicory) but I feel that this would reduce customer satisfaction and hence my own.'

IDEAS IN PRACTICE

Small farm with livestock

Eleanor Hodges has a slightly larger total area of nine acres in a rural area which she works on a rotation system (see page 13) so that five acres are always in production at any one time. Part of this system is a flock of sheep whose main function is to provide the all-important muck to feed the soil. Because 'access to muck' is essential to organic growing, animals are often an indispensable element of a farm.

She sells her produce through a wholesaler and also through her own farm shop. She learned her practical skills in a one day a week, three term general agriculture course at a local agricultural college, having already got a degree in geography.

Growing and tending
Eleanor grows about 45 different items and these include

potatoes, carrots, onions, garlic, peppers, lettuce, cabbage, root fennel, beetroot, parsnips, Swiss chard, spinach and some soft fruit. She also grows a small quantity of herbs. She says that bulk selling of tomatoes and cucumbers especially tend to give a quick return.

She's had the farm for about five years and works it herself with one part-time helper and her husband 'who helps when he can'. They started in spring when they would get the most out of conditions in return for their initial outlay. The land was comparatively cheap because the house had an agricultural restriction on it, meaning that anyone living in it had to be involved in agriculture.

Having good equipment to start with makes an enormous difference for anyone tackling the hardships of converting land into an organic farm. They spent money on a small 'compact' tractor ('which were much cheaper then than they are now') plus a plough and an enormous garden rotavator. They added attachments as they could afford to. They have a large mower because there is grass in the rotation and at certain times of year the animals can't keep up with its growth. Later they bought a second hand full-size tractor because the little one was not big enough to do muck spreading. The large tractor can be used with borrowed machines such as potato planters more easily. They also bought 5.5m × 13.7m (18ft × 45ft) polythene tunnels – whose main disadvantage is that they blow away in high winds and are difficult to insure.

Distribution

'We started small, delivering to some local wholefood shops. They were all interested and their interest generated more interest and more shops.'

Eleanor has considered joining a co-operative but 'We decided it was just not for us. We would have had to sign over 99 per cent of our produce, leaving only a small amount to sell at the garden gate. And we don't want to deprive the local wholefood shops of their one regular supplier of organic produce. Organic growers are fairly rare in these parts.'

THE NITTY GRITTY

Training/ experience
To expect to profit from organically grown produce presupposes a knowledge and understanding of organic gardening or farming. You need to take a practical course in organic gardening, or undertake an intensive period of research, study and practice, or to have spent time growing vegetables on your own organic plot. Any experience of vegetable growing will help.

Obviously, enthusiasm is a must and, from there, anything can be accomplished. There are organisations which can offer information and advice and which publish magazines and manuals and there are colleges offering courses in various aspects of horticulture, agriculture and running a business. See pages 171–2 for further details.

Premises and equipment

If you are content to sell a few surplus vegetables when you happen to have them, then your existing vegetable garden, whether it's a plot in your own garden or a rented allotment, will be sufficient. (In general, however, remember that council allotments are not allowed to be used for making money.)

If you are growing to make a living, then you will need more space than the average domestic garden can provide. One person, with a few machines, could cope with one and a half acres, but this would produce a living supplement rather than a living wage. Anything larger than that will need more than one pair of hands as well as some very sturdy machinery. The cost of land varies enormously depending on where it is, what the soil is like, whether there are agricultural restrictions (as in the case of Eleanor Hodges) and how large the area.

Your checklist should include the following if you want to run a full-time business:

● The land.

● Somewhere to live. (More than one couple I spoke to had started off in a caravan on the site and either built or converted a house in such spare moments as they have had.)

● Horticultural and/or agricultural machinery. This would include a small horticultural cultivator or rotavator for turning over the earth and at least one mower. The more land you have to cope with the more machinery you will need and a small tractor with attachments for digging, harrowing and mowing may be advisable. Advice on such equipment is best sought locally. If you are going to borrow or hire machinery from time to time be sure your tractor is compatible.

● Conventional garden tools: hoe, rake, spade, fork, shovel, hand fork and trowel, string, dibber, secateurs, shears.

● Wheel hoe: 'a piece of intermediate technology wholly appropriate to organic gardening on a small scale' according to Christopher Parker, who uses one himself.

- A greenhouse, which need not be a particularly large one but should be well planned inside with appropriate staging. For a smallholding of several acres you could invest in a large polythene tunnel rather than a greenhouse.
- Wire netting and/or plastic netting.
- Cold frames and cloches.
- Black polythene sheeting or mulch, through which to grow vegetables.
- Bark mulch.
- Supplies of organic manure.
- Bulk fertiliser packs of blood, fish and bone mix or seaweed meal or rock potash.
- Seeds.
- Seed trays and plastic pots.
- A wheelbarrow.
- Watering equipment: hose, sprinkler, watering can, 'seep hose' with holes along its length to keep permanently under polythene mulches and turn on when necessary.
- A strimmer to cut grass right up to trees, posts or walls.
- Plant supports: bamboo canes, wooden stakes, galvanized wire.
- A compost bin.
- Accurate scales for weighing the produce.

Oulets

If you are producing a large acreage of crops, you may find it worthwhile joining a co-operative or you could look for a smaller distributor who will leave you some of your crops to sell locally. Or try a local market, local health food or farm shops, greengrocer or restaurant. Selling from your own stall, garden gate or making small local deliveries to individual customers are also possibilities. It shouldn't be necessary to pretty up the produce with attractive packaging – if it is organically grown, looks healthy and tastes good it will sell from a cardboard box.

Advertising and publicity

If you sell from your garden gate, a notice by the road (see page 160 should be enough to stop passers by and eventually word of mouth should do the rest. If you want to set up your own delivery service, you will have to advertise locally but keep the radius close to home or it won't be worth it in terms of petrol or time expended.

How busy? The small grower is often the packer, sales manager, delivery driver, secretary and director too, yet it is crucial that all of these jobs are done well. Many independent growers are successful in their own terms. One I met has built up a weekly delivery service to over 50 households just through advertising in a local paper and through customers recommending him to their friends. An organic farm of up to four acres will be a full-time occupation for a couple and up to nine acres will need paid help.

What to charge Take local prices as your guideline and price accordingly. Freshly picked organic vegetables may be misshapen but if healthy and unblemished (which they often are) they look better than the cling-wrapped organics sold in super-markets which are often two or three days old. If you charge too much you may find that people buy at first and then lapse and go back to their local supermarket. If you can offer them excellent vegetables at lower prices they could flock to you.

Herbs

Herbs have played an important part in man's daily life from ancient times, when they were used as garden plants, medicines and in cooking. These versatile and delightful plants went out of favour in gardens with the introduction of plant finders' exotics, such as rhododendrons and other large, showy flowers and shrubs and in medicine by modern chemically based drugs.

With the current interest in 'natural' products people are once again turning to herbs. They are a delightful addition to any garden and herb gardens are back in fashion, ranging from the traditional planting of patterned beds to a small herb patch or a few herbs in a windowbox.

Keen herb gardeners aren't content to grow one type of basil or mint but search passionately for unusual varieties. Garden centres tend to stock common ones only, and specialist herb nurseries (selling direct or by mail order) can fill this obvious gap in the market.

How to make money from herbs

The beauty of growing herbs for profit is that you can operate on a scale to suit yourself and just sell a few bunches of herbs to local shops for example, or operate a large mail order company. Here are a few ideas.

Fresh herbs are sold in tiny quantities in shops and supermarkets, and as pot plants in all garden centres. The choice is still relatively small and unimaginative so there may well be a market gap to fill here. It will help to get people interested if you provide a small leaflet on the particular herbs you sell with suggestions for their use. For instance, packet and tinned soups can be transformed by the addition of a few herbs, and a little mint will liven up frozen peas or

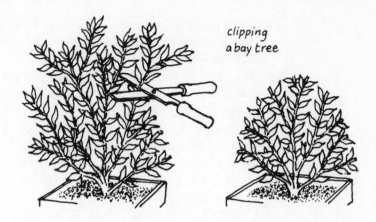

clipping a bay tree

beans. Fennel goes well with fish dishes and basil is delicious with tomatoes. Sweet cicely, angelica, and lemon balm reduce the need for sugar when cooking tart fruits.

Other ideas include selling collections of herbs in large garden pots or window boxes (see page 90). You can use wide, low pots for a collection which might include thyme, chives, sage, golden marjoram and mint.

A large pot or wooden tub looks magnificent with a standard bay tree clipped into shape (see above). Bay is a slightly tender plant. An advantage of having it in a tub is that it can be moved to a greenhouse or conservatory during winter. Bay trees are quite difficult to grow and so can command a high price, particularly if well clipped.

Evergreen herbs such as thyme, hyssop, rosemary and juniper bushes can be sold as decorative plants in tubs and would be attractive as Christmas presents.

Herbs such as pot marjoram, sage, fennel, sweet cicely and lovage can all be used to good effect in flower arrangements because they last so well in water and have particularly pretty foliage.

Alternatively you could set up a mail order herb business (see pages 69–79) and specialise in the more unusual varieties.

A well-stocked and attractive herb garden could be opened to the public for viewing. You could also sell cuttings or pots of herbs or homemade herb jellies and vinegars (see pages 147–152). Or you could serve teas to the visitors (see pages 144–6).

Spin off ideas   All products using herbs should be carefully packaged and labelled.

- Dried herbs can be prettily packaged for cooking (in tiny bags of muslin as bouquets garnis for instance) or for making herb teas.
- They can be put into small pillows to encourage sleep and sewn up into bags for scenting drawers of lingerie.
- Herbs steeped in oils and vinegars make interesting presents for gourmets (see page 148). Herbs can also be used to make different flavoured mustards and pickles.
- Frozen soups could be a useful line to sell as part of the menu for a dinner party. Try sorrel soup, chervil soup, chervil sauce, mint sauce, watercress soup, spinach soup – or even nettle soup, which is still eaten in Ireland but might perhaps appeal more if combined with sorrel, watercress or spinach. Herb mayonnaise and salad dressings are excellent with salads (see page 148).
- Herbs are an ingredient of pot pourris (see page 136).

How to get started

If you already have a few herbs in your garden you can propagate from these by taking cuttings, by root division, collecting seed or in a few cases allowing the plants to re-sow themselves. Some herbs, such as sage, can't be grown from seed and you will have to buy in plants if you don't have one already.

Spring is the best time to plant most herbs and to take cuttings and divide roots. If you are going to sow from seed you will have to begin preparations in autumn (see below).

Sowing for success

Many wild flowers and herbs need to have their seeds subjected to a cold period before they will germinate readily. There are two ways to achieve this. Either sow the seed between late autumn and early winter and overwinter in a cold frame, or put them in the refrigerator.

Sowing outside

Sow the seed in trays using any of the major seed composts, although soil-based composts are often best for autumn sowing because they drain better. Sow the very small seeds on to the surface then water them in. Larger seeds should be covered with compost, equivalent in depth to the diameter of the seed, and watered in. Place the trays in a cold frame or cover with a sheet of glass. During early spring they can be left outside for the sun to bring them on. Germination is often erratic and takes a long period so don't be too eager to prick the seedlings out.

Keeping in the refrigerator

If you don't want to overwinter the seeds, you can simulate winter by putting them into a plastic bag or cover with cling film and store them in the salad compartment of the refrigerator for two to three months.

Seeds that benefit from being treated in this way include the umbelliferae such as sweet cicely (*Myrrhis odorata*), angelica (*Angelica archangelica*) and salad burnet (*Sanguisorba minor*), although angelica and salad burnet are best propagated by root division in spring.

Annual herbs, grown from seed

Chamomile (*Matricaria chamomilla*); nasturtium (*Tropaeolum majus*); parsley (*Carum petroselinum*) – takes five to eight weeks to germinate – borage (*Borago officinalis*); sweet basil (*Ocimum basilicum*), summer savory (*Satureia hortensia*).

Some interesting and rewarding herbs to grow

Angelica (*Angelica archangelica*). Height up to 1.8m (6ft). Hardy biennial or short-lived perennial. Seeds germinate very shortly after harvesting and lose their germination power quickly. Sow as soon as ripe. Likes shade and light soil and dampish position.
Uses: can be used with juniper berries to flavour gin; makes a fresh tasting tea. Stalks can be candied or crystallized. Use in pillows to induce calm. Leaf tips can flavour jams and jellies. Roots and stems are good cooked with rhubarb.

Basil (*Ocimum basilicum*). Height to 45cm (18ins). Hardy perennial in many countries, but treat as annual in temperate ones. Sow directly into pots in spring in greenhouse or indoors. Germination will take 10 to 14 days. Wait until hardened off before transplanting seedlings. Seeds will not ripen for collection unless in a warm climate. Needs warmth and shelter. There are many varieties of basil to specialise in. The very dark purple leaved variety makes a spectacular contrast to other herbs in the garden.
Uses: Good for window boxes or as indoor plants. Many culinary uses, especially good with tomatoes and cucumbers. A handful of leaves steeped in a bottle of wine for several hours makes a digestive tonic and a pot of basil is supposed to get rid of flies.

Bay (*Laurus nobilis*). Height 10m (30ft) or more. Half hardy tree. Propagate by cuttings of half ripe shoots. Grow in sheltered place or even indoors. If grown in tubs can be moved into greenhouse or conservatory during winter.
Uses: dried leaves stimulate appetite and are added to many preserves and to oils and vinegars and marinades.

Bergamot (*Monarda didyma*). Also known as Oswego tea, bee balm. Height 45–90cm (18–36in). Perennial. Named varieties do not come true from seed. Mixed seeds can be sown in cold frame or greenhouse in March. Can also be propagated by division in autumn every two years.
Uses: good added to lemonades or summer drinks. One teaspoonful of dried flowers per cup makes a good tea said to induce sleep.

Common chamomile (*Anthemis nobilis*) also known as Roman chamomile. Height 15–16cm (6–7in). Hardy perennial. Propagate from cuttings of lateral shoots between May and August in equal parts sand and peat in cold frame. Likes sunny situation and well-drained soil.
Uses: chamomile tea (2 tsps flowers to one cup) is supposed to aid digestion and makes a good gargle. Can be used for facial steam baths and as a rinse for blonde hair. Vigorous, non-flowering variety 'Treneague' can be used to make small, scented lawn or path.

Chervil (*Anthriscus cerefolium*) Similar to parsley but more ferny. Height 30–40cm (12–16in). Seeds remain viable for only about one year. Sow in pots from late August to September and maintain a temperature of 7–10°C (45–50°F). Cannot tolerate hot, dry conditions and doesn't transplant well.
Uses: fresh leaves have the best flavour. Makes a good soup and can be used to flavour most foods instead of parsley.

Chives (*Allium schoenoprasum*). Height 10–25cm (4–10in). Hardy perennial. Propagate from seed in spring and root division in autumn. Will grow in sun or semi shade in any fertile soil and does well in window boxes.
Uses: to give mild onion flavour to soups and salads, egg and cheese dishes. Helps to give flavour instead of salt.

Dill (*Peucedanum graveolens* syn. *Anethum graveolens*). Height 45cm (18in). Tender annual. Propagate by seeds and germinate in dark at 15°C. (50°F). Sow from April to June consecutively. Water well.
Uses: use dried seeds and leaves in soups, stews and salads. Helps flavouring in a low-salt diet. Aids digestion.

(Is a powerful laxative so should be taken in small amounts).

Sorrel (*Rumex acetosa*) and **French sorrel** (*Rumex scutatus*). Height 60cm (2ft). Hardy perennial. Divide roots in spring or autumn. Likes light but rich soil in sheltered position in full sun but will tolerate shade.
Uses: makes excellent soup, quiches, good for salads, combined with other herbs.

Sweet Cicely (*Myrrhis odorata*). Height 60–90cm (2–3ft). Hardy perennial. Sow seed in March or April. If dividing roots, cut off the long tapering parts before cutting the rest of the root into sections. Does well in any soil in sun or partial shade.
Uses: roots can be boiled and eaten as a vegetable or in salads. Chopped leaves help to sweeten sour fruit.

Tarragon (*Artemisia dracunculus*). Height 1.5m (5ft). Hardy perennial. Propagate by severing the rhizomes in March or April and replanting. Or take basal cuttings in April and keep at 13–15°C (55–59°F).
Uses: good for flavouring all kinds of food and oils, vinegars and pickles.

Thyme (*Thymus vulgaris*). Height 10–30cm (4–12in). Many different types including variegated and bushy or creeping varieties. Hardy perennial. Propagate by division in March or April or from cuttings of lateral shoots taken with a heel in May or June. Sow seeds in a cold frame in March and April.
Uses: to flavour many foods, as a tea, as a liniment, in bath oils, as a mouth wash.

Picking and drying herbs

Herbs for preserving must be gathered at the moment when they are richest in volatile oils. This is usually from the time the flower buds begin to form until they are nearly open. Exceptions are parsley and chives which can be cut at any time, and sage which develops an unpleasant flavour unless harvested young.

Cut the herbs in the morning on a fine day as soon as the dew has dried. Never collect plants while they are wet. Annual herbs can be cut nearly to the ground but perennials should not be cut too drastically. You may be able to cull from them two or three times during summer. Be careful not to crush or break the herbs when picking or carrying them.

Dry them as quickly as possible in a warm, airy and, if possible, darkened room. The temperature should be between 21°C and 32°C (70°F and 90°F) and never beyond 37°C (100°F). The airing cupboard, a plate warming oven with the doors slightly ajar, near a boiler or in a clean garage with a fan heater would all be suitable drying places. Lay the herbs out on nylon net or muslin for good ventilation. They are ready when the leaves become brittle but before they turn to powder when touched. Once the herbs are dry they must remain dry so they should be allowed to cool and then stored in airtight containers until you are ready to package or use them (see pages 46 and 148–9 for ideas). Do not expose them to light or they will lose their aroma.

IDEAS IN PRACTICE

A small cottage industry

Dove Cottage Herbs is a 'small cottage industry' run by Glyn Onione, an enterprising Welshman, with help from his wife and daughters. He offers a delivery service, delivering the herbs himself. He looks for customers who will take large quantities which makes the service worthwhile, and is willing to deliver large orders several hundred miles away. He backs up his delivery service with mail order. He has a marvellous selection of herbs, many of which you hardly ever come across in garden centres or other nurseries. These include perennial wild basil (*Clinopodium vulgare*), a good collection of thymes, the salad herb 'Good King Henry' (*Chenopodium bonus-henricus*), a very good collection of marjorams, mints, and rosemaries and rue ('shall we say pungent?') as well as most varieties of lavender and many more.

'The busiest periods for herb growing are spring and autumn, which are the major seed growing times for pricking out, though actually I find I am sowing all the year round.'

He aims to have 'one of the most comprehensive lists of herbs and wild meadow flowers available' and can offer plants, seeds or bulbs of about 90 different herbs and three different meadow mixtures.

He has been interested in ecology and plants since his training at the agricultural research station at Woburn Abbey, nearly 20 years ago. Since then he has been the resident gardener of a number of fine country houses.

'I have always gardened organically right from the start and I've always been a conservationist.' This concern for ecological balance is clearly the secret behind the evident and rapid success of his business.

The profits
Glyn thinks it would be easy to make enough money for a new hi-fi or a holiday abroad gardening with herbs. 'You don't need

much space for growing plenty of varieties in pots. You could have 10,000 plants for instance growing in a 6m × 12m (20ft × 40ft) plot. Anything about the size of an average back garden is enough to make a profit. But if you want to make a respectable profit it is much more difficult. You must take into account the advertising costs, administration costs, etc. You might need to move to a half acre site and then you might well need to start paying people for pricking out etc.'

Glyn intends to keep the business on a small enough scale so that he does not expand beyond his enjoyment of the plants. He likes to meet his customers and can advise them on choice of plants for specific situations.

'Most of my customers are either wealthy people with land and money or green-minded and into conservation, like me.'

Advertising

Glyn Onione advertises with 'a few well chosen words' in a few carefully chosen magazines. 'I have wasted a lot of money advertising in the wrong sort of magazines and newspapers. My advice is to stick to reputable, specialised magazines. The best, of course, are booked up in advance and the most respected horticultural magazines may have waiting lists of three months for a four line ad. But just one good contact every now and again is worth the price.' He advertises in several gardening magazines in rotation, 'I may advertise in two separate sections of a magazine, because different sections may catch the eyes of different readers.'

The balance between how much to grow and how much to advertise is difficult. I go for the big sales and advertise as widely as possible.' He has opted for a simple catalogue. 'There's no point in making it too glossy if it means the price must go up.'

Glyn also does all his own accounts but realises that may eventually be no longer practicable 'especially as I shall have to register for VAT, which takes up a lot of time'. He intends to expand a bit, as he has plenty of space for growing and hopes for consistent success but 'on a manageable scale'. He quite clearly loves what he does and is not going to allow making a 'business' out of it spoil things for him.

IDEAS IN PRACTICE

A herb plot

Betty Cole doesn't intend to make a living from her herbs, she grows because she enjoys it and is happy to make a little money.

'Everyone round here grows things, so I just started a herb plot on our 2,000 sq m (0.3 hectares) of wilderness.' Her first plants were thyme, sage, basil and a range of mints. The following year she added lovage, soapwort and rosemary. 'I've tried hyssop which has a pretty leaf and Jacob's ladder. Eau de Cologne mint is delicious in a hot bath though its uses are limited otherwise but it's got such a lovely smell.'

For the first year she sold her herbs at the roadside and intended to offer them to local shops but people very soon get to hear about things in a small community and the manager of the cathedral bookshop suggested selling them through the shop. Betty wasn't sure if this would work but they sold well. She now has a very wide range of herbs.

Growing is very labour intensive and time consuming and Betty has to prick out each plant singly. 'If you were ever to sit down and work out how much you earned in an hour, you would probably die of shock. I'm doing it for the love of it, not to get rich. Living in a small, remote village, I have to keep prices as low as possible. Otherwise people won't buy. But the profits do exist. I probably wouldn't continue otherwise!'

THE NITTY GRITTY

Training/ experience

No formal training is necessary for the successful growing of herbs. Obviously, experience and the knowledge and understanding which develop out of a real enthusiasm are essential. There are many books which can save the beginner from expensive mistakes, but there is no substitute for experience itself.

Herbs are distinct from vegetables and fruit in that customers are likely to be as interested in less usual varieties as common ones, so a good knowledge of a wide range of herbs and their special properties would be an advantage. General advice on the cultivation of herbs and informed suggestions as to their uses in teas, cooking and shampoos and herbal cosmetics will always intrigue potential customers.

Premises and equipment

To grow herbs in pots for selling one doesn't need too much space because they can be dotted around: some indoors, some in the greenhouse, some out in the garden or patio. When supplying plants and/or seeds, a healthy turnover can be made with the produce of only an average sized back garden. A small mail order business might be run from the produce of the garden of a council house (see pages 69–79).

Equipment can be kept to a minimum but you might need

a greenhouse for propagation (though not necessarily a large one). The most important thing is to have a reliable supplier of plants or seeds to begin with. Some means of printing a herb list or catalogue which is neither too glossy (and expensive) nor too cheap and shoddy, should be researched carefully.

Your checklist might include the following:

- Growing area as discussed opposite.
- Office space.
- Greenhouse for propagation, not necessarily a large one.
- Office equipment and stationery: word processor or typewriter; headed paper, order forms, paper for catalogues, etc, if selling by mail order.
- Pots: small plastic pots, or 'polybag' pots or square pots, ten of which will fit into a tray of moulded polystyrene. This makes cultivation and watering easier and packaging too, if you can persuade people to buy in tens. At a pinch, when your enterprise is still very small, you can use yogurt, cottage cheese and ice cream tubs with holes punched in the bottoms, but once you are into greater numbers these are not so satisfactory. They'd certainly be acceptable when selling to friends or at the garden gate.
- Compost for seed growing.
- Compost for potting on.
- Labels (buy in quantity).

Outlets   Your own garden – if conveniently placed for access and parking – car boot sales, craft fairs if oriented towards plants (otherwise don't bother). Mail order customers will come through your advertisements, and perhaps through people who have taken an interest in your wares at specialist plant sales.

Advertising and publicity   If you are selling from your own premises, a notice by the road should attract passers by (see page 160). You can also advertise in the classified columns of local newspapers and in specialist gardening magazines (see pages 159–160).

If you wish to sell culinary herbs to local health food shops or planted-up tubs to local garden centres, it will probably be best to approach the proprietors in person.

How busy? Unless you keep it strictly as a side line, selling when you feel like it to the odd craft fair etc., like all serious gardening activities, it will involve a good deal of your time.

First of all you have the growing, which you would probably be doing in any case but which you will certainly have to expand so that what was a hobby will become much more of a responsibility.

Summer may slacken off a little and leave you time for paperwork, research and perhaps taking a holiday. Winter should be very quiet and offer time for preparing the next year's catalogue and perhaps for a complementary business such as drying herbs and packing them to make a little extra income. They can be put into tiny plastic bags or ceramic pots and you might find a market through similar outlets as 'Preserves' (page 151).

What to charge There is no point in trying to undercut the garden centres or hypermarkets, many of which sell a few potted up herbs. Aim to provide better quality and a more interesting range. Consider making up a package of selected herbs at a slight discount or fix an average price and charge the same for each herb – on some you will lose, on others you will gain. Remain flexible about prices, offering discounts for bulk orders or for smaller plants. Some plants which do not sell in the first year will have grown and matured by the second so you could perhaps even charge more for such herbs as rosemary, lavender, sage, and the mints.

2
FLOWERS AND FOLIAGE

Wild

flowers

'Growing' wild flowers may seem a contradiction in terms. Perhaps many people think of wild flowers as weeds when out of their natural habitat and growing in a garden. However, several factors have made it increasingly difficult for many native species to survive in the wild. These include too prodigal a use of chemical pesticides and herbicides, the cutting down of many hedges and verges which once provided ideal habitats for plants and for the creatures which help to distribute the seed. Also, modern agricultural strains of grasses are very vigorous and overwhelm other plant life.

The present fashion of setting aside a piece of garden as a wild meadow and growing wild species as part of a herbaceous border makes good sense. It protects endangered plants, ensuring their survival and giving us the pleasure of their delicacy and individuality.

Many wild plants attract butterflies and other insects and they have the added charm of being the originals of many of our garden plants. For instance, we can recognise the minute meadow crane's bill as the forerunner of the hardy garden geranium, the starry flowered yarrow as a relative of the great gold-plated achillea, and creeping bellflower as the small relation of the large garden campanulas.

Increasing demand

People are becoming more aware of the importance of conserving wild flowers, and of their charm even in a small garden or in town gardens. There is a good opportunity for selling plants you have grown from seed – particularly since it has become an offence for unauthorised persons to uproot any wild plant without reasonable cause. (An authorised person is the owner or occupier of the land or someone who has his permission.) In Britain certain wild plants are already very scarce and except under licence or under special circumstances no one may uproot, pick or destroy any of them.

Because you cannot pick them in the wild, these plants are not readily available for growing at home. Some garden centres do stock them, but they charge high prices and have a limited range. Once you have bought and grown wild flowers, you can collect the seed and grow more to sell.

There is certainly an opportunity here for supplying plants to keen gardeners. However, there is still much to be learned about the effects of different plants on each other and it only needs one over-vigorous plant to ensure the failure of most of the other species. So some knowledge of wild plants and their habitats and requirements is essential, and it will be helpful to be able to suggest to customers varieties and combinations which will grow well in specific situations.

Seed procedure

The traditional methods of seed sowing, plant division, cuttings and layering are the same for wild plants as for cultivated ones. But seeds do not all take the same length of time to germinate, or flourish under the same conditions, and gardeners who are used to propagating garden cultivars may be dismayed by the slow germination of wild plant seeds.

On pages 60–1 is a list of native species from which seed should never be taken in the wild. Happily there are many other plants whose seeds can be collected for propagation.

Cut the seed stems as soon as they are ripe and carry them home in a plastic bag. Spread them out on a baking tray or plate in a dry place for two or three weeks to complete their ripening. Thereafter, store in a plastic container (plastic 35mm film canisters are useful) in the refrigerator.

Wild flower seeds do not all take the same amount of time to germinate and can be very unpredictable. Probably there are substances in the soil which act on certain seeds to soften their hard outer cases. The answer is to give the seeds conditions as near to their natural ones as possible. Choose varieties which come from a similar situation to that of your garden, and overwinter the seeds in the fridge to mimic winter. Hard seed cases can be scratched on sandpaper before sowing while tough seeds can be slit with a sharp knife to allow moisture to get in and swell the seed. Most pea seeds (everlasting pea for instance), meadow cranesbill

(*Geranium*) and helianthemum should be gently rubbed with coarse sandpaper. Berries and seeds with hard coats can be stratified by laying them on sand, covering them with sand and leaving them to overwinter out of doors.

Sow when the seeds would naturally be settling into the ground. Use John Innes seed compost and sow in containers or specially prepared seed or nursery beds. For seed beds the earth should be dug several times, raked thoroughly until it is very fine and perhaps sprinkled with a layer of fine compost over the top. When the seedlings are large enough to handle put them into individual pots. They can then be brought into a cool greenhouse. Be very patient when waiting for germination – it may take several weeks.

Wild ferns need special treatment too. Those that form several crowns as they grow older can be lifted, divided, pulled or cut apart and replanted. Ferns with rhizomes can be propagated by root pieces planted directly into small pots, sunk into the ground. If you want to grow from spores, you will need steady fingers because the spores are so tiny, and patience because germination may take months.

Protected species

The following plants may not be uprooted, picked or destroyed except under licence or under special circumstances. Removal of any part of these plants is an offence:

Adder's tongue spearwort (*Ranunculus ophioglossifolius*)
Alpine catchfly (*Lychnis alpina*)
Alpine gentian (*Gentiana nivalis*)
Bedstraw broomrape (*Orobanche caryophyllacea*)
Blue heath (*Phyllodoce caerulea*)
Brown galingale (*Cyperus fuscus*)
Cheddar pink (*Dianthus gratianopolitanus*)
Chidling pink (*Petrorhagia nanteulii*)
Diapensia (*Diapensia lapponica*)
Dickie's bladder fern (*Cystopteris dickieana*)
Downy woundwort (*Stachys germanica*)
Drooping saxifrage (*Saxifraga cernua*)
Early spider-orchid (*Ophrys sphegodes*)
Fen orchid (*Liparis loeselii*)
Fen violet (*Viola persicifolia*)
Field cow-wheat (*Melampyrum arvense*)
Field eryngo (*Eryngium campestre*)
Field wormwood (*Artemisia campestris*)
Ghost orchid (*Epipogium aphyllum*)
Greater yellow-rattle (*Rhinanthus serotinus*)

Jersey cudweed (*Gnaphalium luteo-album*)
Lady's slipper orchid (*Cypripedium calceolus*)
Late spider-orchid (*Ophrys fuciflora*)
Least lettuce (*Lactuca saligna*)
Limestone woundwort (*Stachys alpina*)
Lizard orchid (*Himantoglossum hircinum*)
Military orchid (*Orchis militaris*)
Monkey orchid (*Ochis simia*)
Norwegian sandwort (*Arenaria norvegica*)
Oblong woodsia (*Woodsia ilvensis*)
Oxtongue broomrape (*Orobanche loricata*)
Perennial knawel (*Scleranthus perennis*)
Plymouth pear (*Pyrus cordata*)
Purple spurge (*Euphorbia peplis*)
Red helleborine (*Cephalanthera rubra*)
Ribbon leaved water-plantain (*Alisma gramineum*)
Rock cinquefoil (*Potentilla rupestris*)
Rock sea-lavender (*Limonium binervosum*)
Rough marsh-mallow (*Althaea hirsuta*)
Sea knotgrass (*Polygonum maritimum*)
Sickle-leaved hare's-ear (*Bupleurum falcatum*)
Small alison (*Alyssum alyssoides*)
Small hare's-ear (*Bupleurum baldense*)
Snowdon lily (*Lloydia serotina*)
Spiked speedwell (*Veronica spicata*)
Spring gentian (*Gentiana verna*)
Starved wood-sedge (*Carex depauperata*)
Teesdale sandwort (*Minuartia stricta*)
Thistle broomrape (*Orobanche reticulata*)
Triangular club-rush (*Scirpus triquetrus*)
Tufted saxifrage (*Saxifraga caespitosa*)
Wall germander (*Teucrium chamaedrys*)
Whorled solomon's seal (*Polygonatum verticillatum*)
Wild gladiolus (*Gladiolus illyricus*)
Wood calamint (*Calamintha sylvatica*)

What will grow where

Growing wild flowers is a completely different proposition to growing cultivated ones and particular species are often very fussy indeed about where they will grow and what plants they will tolerate as neighbours.

Soil
When growing wild plants, it is best to choose plants which like the soil rather than try to change the soil to suit the plant (a ruse which usually fails).

A great number of wild flower species will grow in neutral or slightly acid soils. If you have different pH readings in different parts of the garden it will widen the scope for the sort of plants you can grow (see Testing the Soil, page 15).

Plants for acid soils

Many acid loving plants are evergreen and most are long-lived. They make good ground cover. Plants which do better in acid soils include:

Bearberry (*Arctostaphylos uva-ursi*) evergreen, prostrate shrub, pink or white flowers in May and June; well drained, light soil in dappled shade.

Bell heather (*Erica cinerea*) evergreen shrub with purple flowers from June onwards; well drained, moist peaty soil.

Bog rosemary (*Andromeda polifolia* 'Minima') with bell-like pink or white flowers in May and June; moist peaty soil in sun or partial shade.

Common wintergreen (*Pyrola minor*) tufted deciduous shrub with waxy white flowers tinged with rose in racemes. Must have acid soil.

Dwarf gorse (*Ulex gallii*) spiny shrub with small bright yellow flowers and characteristic fragrance. Sheltered peaty soil.

Hard fern (*Blechnum spicant*) sturdy evergreen; moist, shady places.

Ling (heather) (*Calluna vulgaris*) evergreen, bushy, purple flowers in July to September; moist peaty soil.

Irish heath (*Erica mediterranea*) evergreen shrub with rose crimson flowers from March to May; likes warm, wet climate and protection from winds.

Ivy leaved bell flower (*Wahlenbergia hederacea*) slender trailing perennial or annual with long, pale blue bell-shaped flowers from July to August; moist, peaty soil.

Pale heath violet (*Viola lactea*) leafy stemmed perennial with largish pale blue flowers from May to June; rich, acid soil.

Plants for wet places

The following will all grow at the margins of ponds or rivers.

Common skullcap (*Scutellaria galericulata*) bright blue flowers with white markings from June to September.

Great willow herb (*Epilobium hirsutum*) tall, downy perennial with purplish pink flowers from July to September.

Sweet flag (*Acorus calamus*) aquatic perennial with green flowers from June to July.

Purple loosestrife (*Lythrum salicaria*) bright red-purple flowers from June to July.

Water forget-me-not (*Myosotis scorpioides*) bright blue flowers with yellow eyes from April to July.

Water mint (*Mentha aquatica cibrata*) lilac or reddish flowers from July to September.

Yellow flag (*Iris pseudocorus*) bright yellow flowers from June to August.

Plants for a herbaceous border

Many wild flowers look charming in a herbaceous border. All the following, for instance, can be incorporated into the garden.

Bladder Campion (*Silene inflata*), ordinary, well drained soil; sun.

Columbine (*Aquilegia vulgaris*), moist but well drained, leafy soil; sun or partial shade.

Common Centaurea (*Centaurium erythraea*), any well drained soil; sunny position.

Common mallow (*Malva sylvestris*), poor, dry soil; sun or partial shade.

Cowslip (*Primula veris*), chalky soil; full sun.

Cuckoo pint or **lords and ladies** (*Arum maculatum* also *A. italicum*), rich soil, partial shade.

Evening primrose (*Oenothera biennis*), any well drained soil; sunny position.

Everlasting pea (*Lathyrus latifolius*), slightly alkaline, light loam; shade.

Flax (*Linum anglicum*), ordinary, well drained soil; sun.

Forget-me-not (*Myosotis arvensis*), moist soil; partial shade.

Foxglove (*Digitalis purpurea*), any soil; partial shade.

Fritillary (*Fritillaria meleagris*), fertile, moist soil or short turf; sun or partial shade.

Heartsease (*Viola tricolor*), any moist, well drained soil; sun or partial shade.

Hellebore (*Helleborus viridis*), deep, well drained, moist soil; shade or partial shade.

Lily of the Valley (*Convallaria majalis*), plenty of leaf mould or compost; partial shade.

Love-in-a-Mist (*Nigella damascena*), any well cultivated soil; sunny position.

Mullein (*Verbascum thapsus*), any well drained soil; sunny position.

Ox eye daisy (*Chrysanthemum leucanthemum*), light, well drained soil; sunny position.

Ragged Robin (*Lychnis flos-cuculi*), any well drained soil; sun or light shade.

Scabious (*Knautia arvensis*), well drained soil; sunny position.

Sea Holly (*Eryngium maritimum*), ordinary, well drained soil; sunny position.

Thrift (*Armeria maritima*), ordinary, well drained soil; full sun.

Wild strawberry (*Fragaria vesca*), any well drained soil; sun or partial shade.

Some wild ferns and foliage plants

Lady fern (*Athyrium filix-femina*) large lacy leaves; leaf mould, semi shade.

Maidenhair spleenwort (*Asplenium trichomanes*) lime loving, well drained site.

Oak fern (*Gymnocarpium dryopteris*) graceful, emerald green; peaty, well drained soil, damp woods and rocky screes.

Quaking grass (*Briza media*) perennial with slender stems and small purple brown panicles; well drained soil, sunny position.

Solomon's seal (*Polygonatum multiflorum*) graceful arching perennial with greenish white flowers from May to June; woods and shady borders.

Tall fescue (*Festuca arundinaceae*) large, coarse tussocks, graceful panicles of flowers, any meadow.

IDEAS IN PRACTICE

A greenhouse

Tracey Duncombe lives in a rural area where for two years she has managed to make a successful, if small, living from her 'Wild Flowers and Herbs' business, selling plants she has grown from seed.

Tracey's most useful assets have been her lifelong interest in country pursuits and a degree in ecology. After taking her degree she could not find a job in conservation, so took a secretarial course and then worked for a year on a community programme for conservation volunteers. During this time she collected wild flower seeds with the intention of selling them in packets, ready to sow. She typed out a list and put an advertisement in the local paper, but there was no response. 'So there I was with all these seeds, and then I had the idea of growing them myself and selling them as plants.'

When Tracey started, she had already taken on a local gardening job and in talking to her employer discovered that there was a real interest in wild plants. 'Otherwise I probably wouldn't have had the idea in the first place.'

She found a large greenhouse nearby which she was able to rent, and to tide her over during the setting-up of her business she joined a government enterprise scheme (see page 165) which paid her a living wage for a year.

Apart from the greenhouse, the rest of Tracey's equipment was acquired very cheaply. She was given all her plastic pots by a local tree nursery. 'You'd be surprised – everyone brings me pots,' she says.

She had a large notice painted, saying simply 'Wild Flowers and Herbs' and set it up where it could be seen from the road whenever the greenhouse was open to visitors.

'I sell mainly to people who visit me here, to a few schools and to the local Parks Department,' she says. She was asked to supply plants one year for the Wild Flower Garden at Chelsea Flower Show.

Tracey Duncombe keeps an album with photographs of each of her plants, taken when at their peak, with good descriptions of their care, treatment, soil preferences etc. Customers can look through this when making their choices and ask any further questions about cultivation and care.

'Pricing is a slight problem. I used to worry if the prices didn't always tally with the catalogue price, but people don't seem to mind. If someone orders a large number of plants or if a plant looks a bit scraggy, I put the price down.'

The best selling season is, of course, spring. By summer sales fall off, people go on holiday and it's a bad time to start planting out anyway. Tracey collects seeds during the summer and then usually takes a holiday herself.

IDEAS IN
PRACTICE

A small cottage industry

Glyn Onione, who features in the herb section (page 52) has a small cottage industry which also specialises in wild flowers. His interest was sparked off in 1978 when he read an article on meadow gardening and thought 'how sensible and practical'. Since then he has tried to incorporate native wild flowers in all his garden schemes. Flowers such as ox-eye daisies, foxgloves, especially the white form, many of the cranesbills, bladder campion, mullein and sea holly can all look delightful when in an informal garden context or even in herbaceous beds.

Glyn is prepared to make a site visit whenever possible because that's the only way he can confidently advise on the best plants for the situation. 'Over the past year we have visited scores of sites up and down the country and met many customers personally.'

THE NITTY GRITTY

Training/ experience

If you are going to propagate plants from seed, you must understand their basic needs. It is *not* necessary to have a degree, like Tracey, but it is vital to have some knowledge of native wild plants and their propagation techniques.

Premises and equipment

You don't need a large greenhouse for wild flowers. You could even get by with a 3.9m × 3.3m (13ft × 11ft) one; most natural species don't need heat in order to germinate.

If you are planning to sell from a table by the garden gate, you might be able to grow enough in your greenhouse or on windowsills indoors, provided they are by east or west facing windows and will get enough light. Or you could use polythene tunnels (see page 21), which are cheaper than buying a greenhouse.

Other essential equipment includes pots and compost. Pots are comparatively inexpensive if bought in bulk, but are often obtainable free from people who no longer need them. Compost should be bought in large bags, or mixed at home.

Seeds can be obtained from specialist seedsmen and seed exchange schemes or collected from your own plants.

You will also need easy access to running water and a hose or watering cans.

When calculating your initial outlay include the cost of printing a price list, photographs and letterheadings and the cost of producing a simple catalogue.

Outlets

Outlets for selling plants can be a bit hit and miss. In peak season an advertisement in the local paper and a good directional notice board by the road may bring several visitors a day and more at weekends.

Small local craft fairs can be useful. Large national fairs are expensive, but if a fair is widely publicised it may be worth attending.

Go to any 'countryside day' or 'ecology week' and any similar events where there are stalls. Try agricultural college open days and sales; village fetes and car boot sales.

If you are selling seed, it is worth approaching county councils, parks departments, and so on directly. One big order of mixed seeds can make up for a dearth of smaller orders in one year.

Mail order can also be a useful outlet. For small operators it may not be worth the time and trouble, but if you expect to do quite a lot of business that way it is important to have a clear idea of the costings and time involved (see pages 69–79).

Advertising and publicity

If you are off the beaten track, a noticeboard advertising your business is crucial (see page 160).

Advertising in local newspapers usually brings results. The classified advertisements are not expensive and are well read.

It is often useful to write to local schools, parks departments, conservation bodies and so on with details of what you do and suggestions for using plants in natural history or ecology lessons or in parks. When selling anything at all unusual, put together a good looking information sheet or pack. The price list can simply be in black and white but it should have a short description of each plant.

How busy?

Time spent on sowing, tending, watering etc. is sporadic throughout the year but fairly intensive while it is going on. Selling time lasts for around three months – while the plants are still young and growing strongly. So for at least six months, during the growing and selling period, the business could be fairly full time.

Once the plants are past their best there is nothing much to do except collect the seeds when they become ripe.

Winter can be spent working out the strategy for the following year and increasing your knowledge of wild flowers.

What to charge

Keep a check on what is charged by local garden centres and hypermarkets which deal in garden produce. They often have a limited supply of potted-up wild flowers at very low prices. However, they cannot provide the variety or the service which you can offer. Be fairly flexible about pricing – lower the price for a weedy looking plant or if a customer is buying several at a time.

Mail order
plant service

It is easy for people to go out and buy popular and commonly grown plants from local garden centres or one of the many professional large nurseries. But there is certainly a mail order market for more unusual plants, including herbs and wild flowers, which are not commonly found at such local outlets. Sending plants by post is an established way of selling, and on the whole plants manage to survive pretty well and customers are satisfied.

Before you start

There are certain inherent problems which you should be aware of before you start.

It is almost certainly best to specialise: in alpines or in a particular form of exotic plant, or in silver-leaved plants or plants from a particular part of the world. You will acquire a deeper knowledge of your plants that way and will be able to join plant societies whose members also specialise. These are good for exchanging ideas and experiences.

It is difficult to know how many plants to grow in the beginning. Build up your mail order customers slowly at first, until you can see how many plants you sell.

It is also difficult to decide how many of *each* plant to grow. Some may be popular one year and unaccountably lose their appeal the following year. The best thing is to indicate in your mail order catalogue if there are limited supplies of a particular plant and ask customers to give second choices.

If you offer a 'package' selection of say ten plants chosen by you at less than the normal cost, it not only attracts buyers but can make the packaging procedure simpler and quicker to manage.

You will have to decide whether you want to use the postal system or some other form of delivery service. On the whole most people find the postal system rather more reliable than any other because at least the postman knows where to find the address, whereas other drivers may give up and leave the plants languishing in the back of the van over a weekend.

You will have to compile a catalogue. This may be fairly hard to do if you are constantly collecting new plants from different sources.

The catalogue

One catalogue a year, in spring, should be sufficient with a supplement in autumn. It need only be a sheet or two of paper, or could be a small booklet.

- Put in the catalogue only the names of those plants you know you will have plenty of.

- Make sure all your plants are well documented and on file. A small computer or word processor will help in your indexing of plants and in typing and printing the catalogue. Failing that, organise a card index system with a card for each plant.

- The catalogue may give common names of plants but should *always* give the correct Latin name, because this is used universally to identify plants and eliminates confusion.

- A short description of each plant next to its name with its place of origin and guidelines to basic soil and site requirements is useful if you have sufficient space.

- Ensure that you include your name and address prominently on the catalogue and give the opening times of your garden, if it is open to visitors. If prices include postage and packing, say so. If not, indicate how much to add for this. Also, state whether prices include VAT, if relevant (see page 168).

- Book the printer early and make sure he can get the catalogue out in good time – at least three weeks before you want to start sending the plants out – preferably earlier to give people time to plan and order. A word processor could be used to run off a few copies but you will almost certainly find it cheaper to use a printer for larger quantities.

Examples of catalogues

The clarity of the information in your catalogue is all important. Here are some samples of the information and 'conditions of sale' from different catalogues.

A catalogue introduction

At the time of writing we are able to offer the plants/seeds/bulbs of about 360 varieties of **native** wild flowers and garden herbs. Our stock is always increasing and given enough notice, we are confident that we can supply most native plants or the seeds thereof. **(We hope it goes without saying that we do not take our plants from the wild, nor do we as a matter of policy offer *any* plants/seeds listed on the schedule of protected plants).** We are still a small family-run nursery despite our having to move to a far larger growing site, which should be able to satisfy all of our needs for the foreseeable future. We offer a personal service and are always pleased to help in any way we can with your problems by letter or phone (we do prefer the latter).

Dove Cottage Herbs

Plant descriptions

Androsace lanuginosa, Wisley variety
Himalayas. A distinct and lovely species with trailing silver-leaved stems and clusters of pale lilac flowers. Cool, gritty soil. Ideal cascading over the edge of a raised bed or trough.

Campanula aucheri
Caucasus. A lovely alpine bell-flower with clusters of rosettes covered with large, short-stemmed blue flowers in summer. Dies down to a thick carrot-like rootstock over winter.

Tim Ingram.

Customers will be grateful for graphic descriptions like these, which tell you where the plant comes from originally (which gives clues to its culture), what it looks like, and how to use it effectively.

Conditions of sale:

1 All seeds and plants are offered subject to availability on receipt of order.

2 Orders will be despatched in strict rotation, usually within 28 days of receipt of order (unless by prior arrangement).

3 If a particular plant is out of stock it will be forwarded on as soon as it becomes available again. If this is unlikely we will give a cash refund.

4 We take great care to maintain a high standard, but if our plants reach you in poor condition please contact us immediately for replacement or a full refund.

5 Cash with order. Cheques/postal orders made payable to ...

Plants to specialise in

You may like to specialise in various types of plant. Choose categories that you are particularly interested in or know a bit about. The following are a few suggestions.

Silver foliage plants

Alchemilla mollis, from Carpathians to Asia Minor. Ordinary, well-drained soil; full sun.

Armeria maritima (thrift), from Europe. Sandy soil; full sun.

Artemisia ludoviciana, from N. America. Ordinary, well-drained soil; full sun.

Artemisia absinthium 'Lambrook Silver', from Europe. Ordinary, well-drained soil; full sun.

Chamaecyparis pisifera 'Cyaneoviridis', from Japan. Moist soils but less happy on chalk; partially sheltered or open position.

Centaurea dealbata, from the Caucasus. Well-drained soil; sheltered position.

Hosta sieboldiana, from Japan. Moist garden soil; sunny or shady spot.

Ruta graveolens (rue), from S. Europe. Any well-drained soil, does well on chalk; sunny position.

Santolina chamaecyparissus (Lavender cotton), from S. France. Any well-drained soil; sunny position.

Sedum cauticola (stonecrop), from Japan. Any well-drained soil; sunny position.

Sedum sieboldii medio-variegatum, from Japan. Any well-drained soil; sunny position.

Stachys olympica 'Silver Carpet' (woundwort, betany), from the Caucasus to Iran. Ordinary well-drained soil; sunny position.

Zauschneria californica (Californian fuchsia), from California and Mexico. Sandy loam, well-drained; sunny position.

Alpines and dwarf perennials

Ajuga reptans (bugle), from Europe. 'Burgundy glow', 'Tricolour', or 'Atropurpurea' and variegata. Any ordinary soil; sun or shade.

Anemone polyanthes, from the Himalayas. Ordinary soil with plenty of leaf mould; sun or partial shade.

Aquilegia scopulorum (columbine), from N. America. Sandy loam enriched with leaf mould; sun or light shade.

Iberis sempervivens (candytuft), 'Little Gem', from S. Europe. Light, sandy loam; full sun.

Pulsatilla vulgaris (pasque flower), from Europe. Chalky soil; open sunny position.

Sedum spurium (stonecrop), from the Caucasus and N. Iran. Any well-drained soil; sunny position.

Plants for winter interest

Betula pendula 'Youngii' (weeping birch), from Europe and Asia Minor. Prefers acid soil but will grow on chalk; sun or partial shade.

Cornus alba (dogwood), from Siberia and N. Korea. Bright red winter bark. Damp soil; open or shady position.

Cornus stolonifera 'Flaviramea' (dogwood), from N. America. Bright yellow winter bark. Damp soil; open or shady position.

Daphne mezereum (daphne), from Europe and Asia Minor. Pink flowers from February to April. Loamy soil, well-drained in winter, moist in summer; likes lime; open, sunny position.

Forsythia ovata (golden bells), from Korea. Yellow flowers in February. Any garden soil; sun or light shade.

Helleborus argutifolius (hellebore), from Corsica and Sardinia. Evergreen with pale green flowers from March to April. Rich, loamy soil, well-drained; shade.

Helleborus niger (Christmas rose), from Central and S. Europe. Pinkish white flowers from December to March. Rich, loamy, well-drained soil; shade.

Iris danfordiae (dwarf iris), from E. Turkey. Bright yellow flowers from January to February. Well-drained limey soil; sunny position.

Iris reticulata (dwarf iris), from Russia. Deep purple flowers in February and March. Well-drained, limey soil; sunny position.

Evergreen plants for hedges

Berberis darwinii (barberry), from Chile. Medium growth rate. Any well-drained soil; any position except dense shade.

Buxus sempervirens (box), from Europe. Slow growing. Ordinary or chalky soil; open or shady position.

× *Cupressocyparis leylandii* (Leyland cyprus). Fast growing hybrid. Ordinary soil; open or partly-shaded position.

Escallonia macrantha, from S. America. Medium rate growth. Well-drained, lime-free soil; warm, sheltered position.

Euonymus japonicus (spindle tree), from Japan. Slow growing. Any garden soil; sunny or shady position.

Fagus sylvatica (beech), from Europe. Slow for two years then medium growth; leaves turn brown in winter. Sandy or chalky and gravelly loam; open position.

Ilex aquifolium (holly), from Europe and N. America. Slow growing. Ordinary garden soil; sun or shade.

Lavandula spica (English lavender), from Mediterranean regions. Slow growing. Well-drained garden soil, good on chalk or limestone; sunny position.

Ligustrum ovalifolium (privet), from Japan. Fast growing. Ordinary garden soil; sun or shade.

Lonicera nitida (honeysuckle), from China. Fast growing. Ordinary garden soil; shade for roots, sun for top growth.

Rosmarinus officinalis (rosemary), from S. Europe and Asia Minor. Medium growing. Well-drained soil; sheltered sunny position.

Taxus baccata (yew), from Europe and N. Africa. Slow growing. Any soil, sunny or shady position.

Packaging   Plants for sending in the post should be compact and sturdy. Large plants are more likely to get damaged in the post and will need more packaging. Plants travel best in their pots, so that their roots are disturbed as little as possible.

No manufacturer seems yet to have provided specific packaging to fit round small plastic pots. There is some good moulded polystyrene packaging for the very tiny peat pots, which is used by large seed suppliers, and it would be helpful if something similar were available for the rather larger pots that most nurserymen dispatch their plants in. Even large, well-established nurseries have to resort to second hand boxes. The best solution at present does indeed seem to be to use cardboard boxes and newspapers.

Wrapping plants for posting

1 Roll the plant up in its pot in a large format newspaper.

2 Make a small tuck at the bottom under the pot and gently fold the paper over the top, which leaves the plant space to breathe, but provides a fairly firm support. If the plant may be two or three days in transit, cover the whole with a plastic bag and seal so that the moisture is conserved.

3 Pack the pot or pots securely into a cardboard box, filling any gaps with scrumpled newspaper. Seal up the box with heavy duty 2cm (¾in) wide plastic tape.

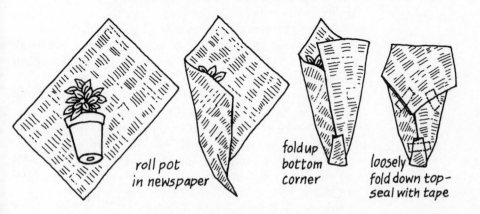

roll pot in newspaper

fold up bottom corner

loosely fold down top – seal with tape

Note: It is particular difficult to package securely in spring when the roots have not yet grown enough to fill the pot and bind the compost. So in that season make doubly sure the plants cannot move around in their packaging and if necessary tape newspaper over the pot to hold the compost in place.

- Large plants and plants sent in wet soil weigh much more than small dry ones and therefore cost more to post. So pack plants while still small, if possible, and when the soil is on the dry side but not completely dried out. If plants are larger, let the soil dry out a little and wrap the plant and pot in polythene to conserve the moisture.

Posting
Before you send out your first batch of parcels, you should get in touch with the post office who may have a special deal for people setting up new businesses by which the first so many parcels can be sent free of charge. They may also have advice about packing and weighing parcels.

- Parcel post is quite rapid and satisfactory for some people; others prefer first class letter post as the parcels tend to get battered.

- Make sure you work out the postage correctly. If you miscalculate the weight of your plants or use rates from last year, or from other people's catalogues (who may be sending smaller and therefore lighter plants than you), you may be seriously out of pocket.

- Encourage clients to accept plants only in autumn or spring. Planting is much less likely to be successful in summer, so you are more likely to have dissatisfied customers.

- To simplify costing consider charging a fixed price for all plants. This works with some plants to the customers' advantage, with others to the supplier's, but on average it is simple and fair.

- Even the postal system is not always reliable and many plantsmen worry about sending parcels when there is a postal strike in case they suffer by being too long in their boxes. It is essential to work out 'safe' posting dates so that plants don't languish in boxes over a week-end, say, especially a bank holiday one. This means only posting on the first three days of the week (or on the first two days of the week before a bank holiday).

Watering systems

You can propagate an enormous number of plants in quite a small greenhouse. There are watering systems which will save a good deal of labour and keep your plants alive if you are away. Self-watering pots contain a reservoir at the base. This will hold enough water to keep the plant alive for

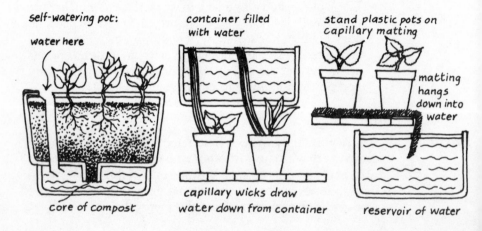

self-watering pot:

water here

core of compost

container filled with water

capillary wicks draw water down from container

stand plastic pots on capillary matting

matting hangs down into water

reservoir of water

about three or four weeks, unless they are in a very warm position. The reservoir is filled through a hole near the base, or through a tube just above the surface of the compost. The pot may have a water level indicator. The water reaches the compost by a capillary system such as a wick of fibrous matting or a stick of compressed fibres or a core of compost.

Self-watering pots are pretty expensive and if you have many plants to water, simple capillary wicks or matting would probably be better. The wicks draw water from a filled container to the tops of pots standing at a lower level. Capillary mats have one end hanging down into a reservoir so the whole mat is constantly saturated. The plastic pots sit on the mat and draw up water as they need it. This system is most efficient with clay pots.

One other method is to water the pots and then immediately cover them with half of a plastic lemonade bottle (see above left). The large bottles just fit round the rim of 7cm (3in) pots. This is good for small numbers. An alternative is to use plastic bags supported on four thin stakes and taped round the pots (see left). This will keep the moisture in for two or three weeks. Don't let the bag touch the foliage and keep out of direct sunlight.

IDEAS IN PRACTICE

A small mail order business

Tim Ingram has been collecting and growing plants since he was 15. Both his parents were involved in horticulture and Tim is now operating his small business from 6,000 sq m (an acre and a half) of what used to be an old cherry orchard behind their house.

At university he studied plant physiology and then worked on research into plant growth regulators. He gave up laboratory work in 1986 to join a government enterprise scheme and began selling unusual plants which he propagates from seed. His plants originate from all over the world and in particular he specialises in those of New Zealand and Australia, including a collection of Eucalyptus.

Among the alpines and dwarf and herbaceous perennials he offers *Codonopsis viridis* from the Himalayas, *Cotula astrata luteola* from New Zealand, *Eryngium agavifolium* from Argentina and *Salvia patens* from Mexico. Among the trees and shrubs he offers *Callistemon linearis* from Australia, *Cassinia fulvida* from New Zealand, twenty different Hebes, *Helichrysum bellidioides* from New Zealand, *Sorbus reducta* from N. Burma and W. China. 'I am fortunate in that the soil here is superb; fertile and very deep. It holds the moisture yet is well drained so I can change the conditions and easily grow lime haters as well as lime lovers.' He believes that a large range is the secret of success and tries to avoid growing too many of one species.

Although Tim sells largely by mail order, he would like to encourage more people to visit the garden. Visitors are well rewarded by a green carpet of lawn on a slope laid out in curved and generous beds with a wealth of visual surprises, including unusual colour combinations and a small silvery copse of varieties of eucalyptus sheltered in the dip. The garden is already open under the National Gardens Scheme on specific days and the nursery is open every day from 2 to 6pm except Monday and Friday.

'This year I've had 500 requests for catalogues but I also take plants to local car boot plant sales and sales held by the Alpine Garden Society of which I am a member.' (See page 171 for addresses.)

He would like to buy more land – perhaps 20,000 to 24,000 sq m (2 to 2.5 hectares) – to give a more satisfactory area from which to sell plants and to set up propagation space. As it is he thinks he may have to specialise in smaller plants such as alpines – a high value crop which doesn't take up much space.

THE NITTY GRITTY

Training/ experience

Experience is important if you wish to grow plants to sell. Some training in plant physiology, ecology and cultivation of plants would also be useful. You need to be capable of succeeding with both seeds and cuttings, and the plants for sale must be strong and healthy. It takes time to build up contacts for seed and plant supplies, and when compiling a catalogue it helps to be familiar with plant species, their environments and their nomenclature (taxonomy).

Premises and equipment

You will need a greenhouse but it need not be an enormous one to begin with. If you are growing hardy perennials you won't need much heat. (Heating can be very expensive.) The more species you want to offer and the more you expect to sell, the more space you will need for seed boxes and cuttings, propagators, peat, sand and compost.

You will also need 'office' space for filing, indexing, answering letters and packing parcels.

You will initially have to buy plants and seeds until you are able to propagate from existing stock. Cost out the processes involved in compiling the catalogue, stationery, packaging and postage (though this you will get back via the charge you make to your customers). Seed societies and seed exchanges are a good source of quality seeds (make sure you, in turn, provide good quality ones).

Outlets

Your outlet is mail order and your main customers will be individuals who are genuinely interested in the sort of plants you grow.

Advertising and publicity

If you are offering unusual plants advertise in appropriate specialist magazines. One advertisement in each of two specialist magazines might bring in around 500 replies. Each enquirer should be sent a catalogue and you can expect about ten per cent of these to buy plants.

Keep a record of who you send catalogues to so that you can build up a mailing list and send catalogues automatically next year.

Another useful way of getting business is by word of mouth and by being seen at plant sales and meetings of plant societies.

Your advertising should stress that you are offering an interesting range which is different from standardised garden centre products.

How busy?

If you are doing only mail order with no garden open, you will have spurts of seasonal orders in spring and autumn which will keep you busy packing. However, you will have to be caring for plants, nurturing, potting on, watering etc. most of the year. During summer you may also want to attend plant sales as suggested earlier. In winter you will be preparing the catalogue for spring, cleaning out the greenhouse and equipment.

What to charge

It's difficult to say what you should charge for unusual plants. The best plan is to look at other catalogues of a similar nature and price in step with these.

Selling
cut flowers

It never occurs to most people who enjoy gardening and love their plants and flowers to try and find a market for them. In fact, many healthy herbaceous and shrubby plants grow all the better for being picked, obligingly producing more and more blooms. If you concentrate on plants for their abundance of flowers rather than for their foliage, even after you've filled every vase in the house with fresh flowers you may still have plenty left to pick and sell. To take a few examples, sweet peas, asters, chrysanthemums, marigolds (*Calendula* and *Tagetes*), daffodils, *Gaillardia*, *doronicum*, Sweet William, pinks and carnations are all free flowering, brightly coloured and long lasting in the garden (as well as in vases).

Most of the daisy-like flowers and many silvery foliaged plants last well in water. These include rue (*Ruta graveolens*), *Stachys lanata*, *Eucalyptus gunnii* and most of the *Artemisias*. Hosta leaves, *Fatsia japonica* leaves and ferns are also good for flower arrangements.

Seasonal blooms

If you want to be able to cut flowers almost all year think about restocking your garden. The following seasonal blooms are all worth considering.

Spring flowers
Pansies, primulas, narcissus, grape hyacinths, hellebores, forget-me-nots, bleeding hearts (*Dicentra spectabilis* and *Dicentra formosa*), scillas, tulips, lungwort (*Pulmonaria*), sweet violets (*Viola odorata*), forsythia can all be sold in small bunches. Taller stems could include: tulips, narcissus,

mallow, viburnum, spiraea, rosemary, decorative cherry (*Prunus*), camellia, magnolia, euphorbia.

Summer flowers
Iris, roses, polygonum, lily of the valley, thrift, stock, achillea, delphinium, lupin, lilies, gladioli, cornflowers, catmint, mock orange (*Philadelphus*), lilac, lavender, gypsophila, freesia.

Autumn flowers
Scabious, dahlia, rose hips, limonium, acanthus, lilies, hydrangea, aster 'Novae-Angliae', China aster (*Callistephus chinensis*), pyracantha berries.

Winter flowers
Snowdrops, Christmas rose, holly berries, winter jasmine (*Jasminum nudiflorum*), mahonia, cotoneaster.

When to pick

Some flowers are much longer lasting than others when cut and it is important to pick them at the right stage. Flowers should be picked when not quite open, early in the morning and never during rain. Daffodils can be picked when quite tightly in bud and will open gradually and flower for a long time.

Immediate treatment of cut flowers

There are ways of treating specific flowers which will help them to last longer. This is an important consideration if they are to be transported and perhaps kept on display for some time before being sold.

- As soon as you bring the flowers in, even if you have only just cut them, cut the stems again, at an angle so that as much of the stem is exposed as possible. Strip all the lower leaves from the stems to prevent them from rotting and contaminating the water.

- The bottom section of green stems should be scraped with a knife or scissor blade so that they can more easily take up water (geums, hyacinths).

cut stems at an angle

remove lower leaves

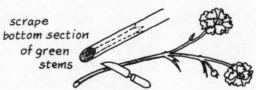
scrape bottom section of green stems

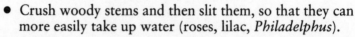

- Crush woody stems and then slit them, so that they can more easily take up water (roses, lilac, *Philadelphus*).
- Hollow stems (lupins and delphiniums) should be held upside down while you pour water into them. When full, plug the stems with a piece of wet cotton wool or kitchen tissue and stand them in water immediately.
- Milky stems (euphorbia, poppies, fennel) should be singed with a flame.

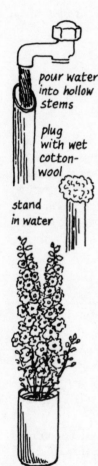
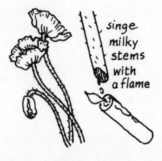

- Most herbaceous and woody flowers will respond well if you plunge the stems in hot water before using them in arrangements; this may also revive wilting blooms (buddleia, acanthus, hollyhock, laburnum, malva, sunflower, wormwood (*Artemisia absinthium*).
- For selling at a stall or by the garden gate, stand the bunches in water in old containers, or wrapped in paper with the base of the stems wrapped in wet cotton wool. Try and keep them in the shade.

Transporting cut flowers Transport blooms with their stems wrapped in wet cotton wool and then plastic bags. Or carry them in tall, narrow containers – a bucket for many flowers, a vase for fewer. Make sure that the containers are well supported, and protect the flower heads from damage.

IDEAS IN PRACTICE

A front garden

Rose Vesey lives in a red brick bungalow just a garden's length away from a narrow, winding country road which leads to a village in one direction, to a hypermarket in the other. Many cars use the road, and they have to drive fairly slowly. As there is off-road parking Rose is in an ideal position to set up a small table and sell cut flowers. She puts together colourful bunches of pinks, oranges, reds and yellows which attract passers-by without any need for a notice.

Rose Vesey's front garden is about 2 sq m (20 sq ft). In it she grows a riotous medley of herbaceous and annual blooms, including marguerites, phlox, peonies, dahlias, sweet peas and marigolds. She is a natural gardener, until recently growing entirely for her own enjoyment. She started selling quite by accident, when her sister was due to come on a visit from Canada. Mrs Vesey wanted her to see the marvellous show of sweet peas while it was still at its best. 'Someone told me that if I picked the flowers they would grow even better, so I started to pick them in order to keep them flowering until my sister arrived. I didn't know what to do with all the flowers I'd picked so I started putting them outside the front gate on a small table. I put a little pot beside them with a notice giving the cost – just a token amount really – and they sold like hot cakes.'

Rose can see the road from her window and can come out pretty smartly to collect the money or have a chat with her customers.

'On the whole people are very honest. Quite often, if they haven't the exact change for the flowers, they will put a coin of a higher value into the pot. We did have some stolen once. Several bunches and the pot they were in. But I think I know who took them and I haven't had any more trouble.

'It's quite surprising how much you make over a summer. Last year I made enough money to buy a video recorder.'

Rose's husband grows beans and vegetables in their back garden and they have now started selling beans as well. 'These are fresh and tender, and cheaper than you'd buy anywhere else locally so they also sell very quickly. I have a freezer, but I'm too lazy to freeze much,' Mrs Vesey says.

THE NITTY GRITTY

Training/ experience

No training is needed but you do need to know how to keep your plants happy: well watered, well fed, healthy and unblemished, with large blooms over a long period.

Premises and equipment

All you need is a large enough bed for a plentiful supply of flowers. If your garden seems too small, remember that climbers such as jasmine, clematis and roses can provide a good number of flowers and sweet peas can be trained up a pyramid or wall trellis.

If you do not have a garden, an allotment will do, or an elderly neighbour might be glad for you to tend his or her garden, rather than have it sadly deteriorate.

If selling from the garden gate you will need a small table or bench covered with a showerproof cloth. It's best to have the table in shade; if you have no shade put up a sun umbrella. You will also need a few large jars and a small tin for money and that's it. Rescue the flowers if it starts to rain.

If selling to florists you will need transport.

Outlets

The obvious one is your own garden gate, if you get enough passing trade. It is best if you can view the table from your window or sell from a small outhouse or garage.

Local florists may be glad of really fresh flowers of a type they can't get from the big suppliers and are often quite willing to take small quantities. Go to your local florists and see what they are selling and, particularly, what they have not got. Then ask whether they would be interested in the more unusual ones you have to offer. You will do best if you have flowers, foliage or berries you can pick all year round (see pages 80–81). Not only will you have regular money coming in but you will be able to keep up contact with your clients.

Local hotels and restaurants might be interested. You could offer to do the flowers for the dinner tables in a restaurant – but this involves a commitment to keeping a good supply and making sure the table arrangements are always fresh, so think twice before leaping.

Flower arrangers and flower arranging circles may be interested in particular types of flower. If you are skilled at flower arranging, you could do arrangements for weddings and parties etc. (See 'Flower Arranging', pages 122–130).

Local flower arranging societies may be worth approaching or even joining in order to find customers.

Advertising and publicity

For garden gate selling or selling to shops, you don't need to advertise. It is a question of knocking on doors to find suitable outlets and customers. If you did have a huge quantity of sweet peas, say, the chances are that the local florist would take them all anyway.

How busy? Unless you build up a commitment to provide a constant supply, the nice thing about growing your own flowers for cutting is that you can be as busy or leisured about it as you please. If you go away you might need somebody to come and water your plants, but you'd probably organise that even if you were not selling any.

There may be deliveries to make to your customers, but that need not be a burden. You would probably combine delivering the flowers with a shopping trip in town.

What to charge For flowers sold at the front gate, the price would need to be rather less than for flowers bought in a shop because your overheads are minimal and part of the attraction for the customer is the 'bargain' element.

When selling to a florist the best thing is to negotiate with the shop manageress, who will have a pretty good idea of what your flowers will be worth to her. And if you keep a check on what they are sold for, you can decide for yourself whether it is worth your while.

For supplying hotels and restaurants, ask around discreetly and find out who is doing a similar service locally, and try to discover what they charge. Keep your prices at a similar level. Undercutting rivals by too much is not a good idea; it will cause bad feeling and could start a 'price war' in which only the retail outlet is a winner. However, giving a better service for slightly less money is a good idea.

Container
gardening

Container gardening has become popular for many reasons. It is a good way of having a 'garden', however miniature, on a patio or balcony. It is useful to put tender plants outside in containers in summer and be able to bring them in in winter. It is convenient to grow plants in containers in a 'courtyard' garden or to grow where you don't want the extra work of a lawn or flower beds. It is a good way of bringing colour to a street front. It provides an opportunity to grow plants not suited to your garden soil, for example camellias and rhododendrons if you have chalky or alkaline soil.

A container garden can be anything from a small tub or pot of seasonal flowers to a large tub of permanent evergreen plants or small trees, or a window box or hanging basket of cascading plants.

Getting started

The advantage of container gardening is that you can begin at any time of year. Also you can operate on a scale to suit yourself. You may just want to sell a few hanging baskets to friends, or you may want to build up a large business supplying garden centres as well as selling direct.

To start with you need to buy containers and/or hanging baskets which you can then plant up with young plants that you have propagated from existing stock or seeds, or bought wholesale. They are offered for sale when the plants have matured. You will be making a profit on the container and the plants, as well as charging for your time and design skills.

Customers may have special requirements, such as pots for a very sunny corner or a shady basement patio. If working on a small scale you can simply take orders for special requirements. On a larger scale you could stock planted containers suitable for a variety of different conditions (see pages 88–9).

The business could be expanded by offering a replanting service. Each season faded plants could be replaced with new ones. The replanting could take place on site (for fixed window boxes and heavy tubs) or you could simply swop the old container or hanging basket for a similar one already planted up.

Choosing containers

Containers must be large enough for the plants to grow comfortably. A 30cm (12in) diameter container would hold several small bedding plants or a small shrub; a 45–60cm (18–24in) container would be more suitable for a large shrub or small tree.

Pots, tubs and window boxes are available in a variety of materials, sizes and shapes.

- Heavy containers of stone or concrete are too dangerous to be placed on a window sill, and unless you are going to plant them up in situ, you will have the problem of lifting and transporting them.

- Fibreglass and plastic containers have the advantage of being light but are still strong enough to support the weight of soil and water.

- Terracotta containers are attractive but heavy and not always frost proof (standing them on wooden blocks or bricks may prevent frost damage). Terracotta containers dry out quickly in wind and hot weather and plants will require more frequent watering.

- Untreated wooden window boxes warp and rot quickly unless they are made of hardwoods such as teak, elm or oak. Before planting in a wooden box, paint the outside and treat the inside with a non-poisonous preservative.

- Tubs may also be made of oak or teak and some are made from large casks sawn in half. They can be fixed on castors to make them easier to move.

- Other container ideas include: second-hand fireclay sinks, chimney pots and wall pots.

Choosing plants

Planting containers with plants that will look good over a long period is something of an art. You must choose plants which will remain lush and in flower for the longest possible time. And in combining different plants, you must choose those which will complement each other and thrive under similar conditions.

- In summer ivies will provide a good green foil to a choice of trailing and upright pelargoniums, petunias, trailing lobelia, nasturtiums, coleus, *Cineraria maritima* or fuchsias. All of these have a very long flowering or colourful period and should look good right into autumn.
- Annuals and perennials which have a very long and free flowering season include pansies, marigolds and tagetes.
- A container herb garden can be made to have a pretty long season, especially if you include some evergreens such as rosemary and sage. See 'Herbs', beginning on page 44.
- For a spring show plant bulbs such as tulips, narcissus and hyacinth.
- Containers for winter interest should include evergreens (see page 89).
- Very small trees can look good with 'ground cover' plants like alyssum or lobelia beneath them.
- Some vegetables can be container grown (see page 36).
- Alpines can look good in small tubs and window boxes. Perennials include: primulas and auriculas, saxifrages, bleeding hearts (*Dicentra spectabilis*), *Campanula cochlearifolia* and dianthus.

Planting suggestions

Pots for summer colour

- Pink *Begonia semperflorens*, blue *Lobelia erinus* with silvery, feathery *Artemisia* 'Powis Castle'.
- Purple hydrangea 'Royal Marine' with pink antirrhinums and silver-leaved *Cineraria maritima*.
- Petunias with cascading variegated ivy.
- A pot full of nasturtiums; another full of pansies.

Pots for a sunny spot

- *Eryngium* and *Echinops*, metallic blue, tall and spiky, with silver *Senecio* 'Sunshine' and pink prairie mallow (*Sidalcea malvaeflora*).
- Lavender and pelargoniums or wild strawberries.

Pots for shade

- Lenten rose (*Helleborus orientalis*) with primulas in front.
- Various ferns with tiny pink or white *Cyclamen hederaefolium* syn. *neapolitanum*, which flower in late summer.

Pots for spring

- Forget-me-nots with tall tulips growing through.
- Species tulips, pasque flowers and rosemary.

Evergreens

Evergreens look good in containers. They can often be clipped to give a formal look to the front of a house. For instance identical pots outside a front door can contain matching clipped bay trees (see page 45), cone-shaped dwarf conifers or clipped box or yew. These are all slow growing and will take some years to reach saleable size, but are worth a lot of money once large enough.

Suitable evergreens for containers include *Fatsia japonica* (often bought as a house plant, but perfectly hardy out of doors), holly, small leaved ivies, hydrangeas, yuccas, box, camellias (lime haters but quite hardy if they don't get the early morning sun after frost), dwarf conifers, dwarf rhododendrons, and large herbs such as rosemary.

Plants for individual planting

You may like to specialise in particular plants. All the following offer wide scope as there are so many different varieties.

- Fuchsias: any well-drained soil with lots of leaf mould and a little bonemeal. Water frequently in dry weather. For bushy plants with lots of flowers, keep pinching back the tips. Fuchsias are also suitable for hanging baskets (see 'Ideas in Practice' on page 92).
- Heathers: grow in peaty soil. Most are lime haters. Winter flowering ones are the brightest.
- Hostas: moisture-retentive soil and shady site. They are usually grown for their attractive foliage but they do flower.
- Hydrangeas: good, loamy, moisture-retentive soil enriched with compost. Mid or partial shade.
- Rhododendrons: will not tolerate chalk or lime and like well-drained, sandy loam. Sheltered, semi-shaded position. Never allow to dry out.

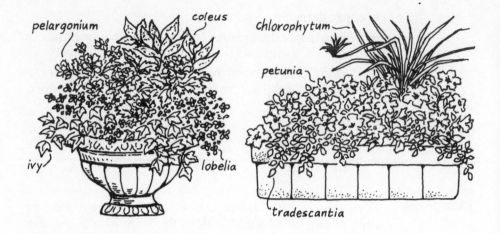

pelargonium
coleus
chlorophytum
petunia
ivy
lobelia
tradescantia

Planting containers

When planting try to get a contrast of heights, foliage and shape as well as colour.

The trailing plants should go in the front of a window box and round the edge of a tub (ivies, trailing lobelia, trailing pelargoniums and tradescantia, for instance). Then the colourful, shortish plants (such as petunias, non-trailing pelargoniums, some fuchsias, alpines and low growing bulbs) and last of all at the back of a box or in the centre of a tub the taller plants to give the added height (tall pelargoniums, tall strap-leaved plants such as *Setcreasea purpurea, Chlorophytum, coleus*). You will have to experiment because pelargoniums may be tall or low growing depending on the variety, and a well-grown fuchsia may provide all the high, middle and trailing levels by itself, or could be planted with *Tradescantia albiflora* to give it a lace petticoat.

There are two methods of planting containers. You can remove the young plants from their flowerpot and plant them in the compost. Alternatively you can put the flowerpots straight into the container and surround them with soil and damp peat. This latter methods makes it easier to change the plants during the season. It also makes it possible for tender plants to be brought into a greenhouse in winter and put outside again when the weather gets warmer.

How to fit a window box

If you are supplying window boxes to a hotel or office, for example, they may require you to fit the boxes as well as plant them.

As the boxes are heavy when filled with soil, place in position before filling them. If placed on a window sill make sure they fit the space snugly. Make the box secure with wedges driven between the ends of the box and the side walls, or with hooks on the box fastened to eyelets in the window frame. Use two wooden blocks to raise the box above the sill. Place a metal drip tray beneath the holes.

If there is no window sill the box can be fixed to the outside wall on strong brackets.

Hanging baskets

Hanging baskets are very popular; you can scarcely pass a home, shop or public building without admiring the mini gardens hanging along its front wall. The secret of successful hanging basket displays is in growing plants which will put forth many flowers in all directions so that you have a wonderful mophead of colour.

Plants which are particularly effective in hanging baskets include dwarf sweet peas (which also smell delicious); variegated-leaved nasturtiums; purple, rather than the more usual blue lobelia; small-leaved, variegated ivies; fuchsias; *Cineraria maritima* with their pretty silvery leaves; *Helichrysum plicatum*; ivy-leaved pelargoniums; *Impatiens; Coleus*; and trailing begonias.

Hanging baskets look very pretty planted with one colour. Green baskets, for example, can be planted with a variety of ivies or herbs (avoid mint, which would take over in no time).

Planting a hanging basket

The original type of wire basket lined with moss dries out quickly and drips when watered. It is possible now to line the basket with a circle of polythene. This will preserve moisture and won't drip as much. You will have to make a few holes in it first to allow for some drainage. You can also buy moulded plastic hanging pots with a drip tray attached. You can of course, use many other receptacles such as an old but pretty enamel casserole, provided it has adequate drainage and you can find a way of hanging it.

If using a traditional basket, rest it in a large flowerpot to stop it rolling around while you are working on it. Line it with sphagnum moss pressed into the mesh. Then put the perforated polythene sheet over the moss. Instead of moss and polythene you could line the basket with a foam sponge liner. This is a sponge circle slit at intervals so that it will

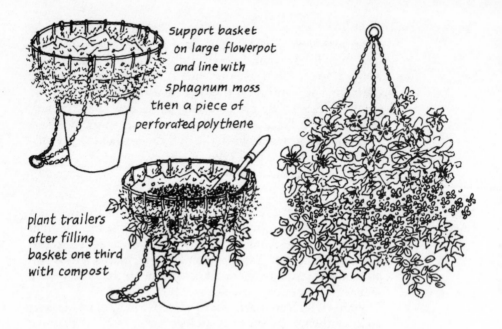

Support basket on large flowerpot and line with sphagnum moss then a piece of perforated polythene

plant trailers after filling basket one third with compost

plastic pot with drip tray

overlap and fit any basket. It will hold water without becoming waterlogged.

Fill the basket one third with compost and plant a few plants (trailers if you are using them) through the sides of the basket so the stems come through the moss or sponge. Now add more compost and position the other plants – shortish plants around the top edge and taller plants in the top centre of the basket. When the basket is completed the soil level should remain about 2.5cm (1in) below the top of the moss.

The biggest problem with hanging baskets is the need for constant watering. Half bury little plant pots in the soil which can be filled with water quickly and will let the water out slowly. Certain plants like Busy Lizzies (*Impatiens*) must be properly soaked, though most pelargoniums will survive in drought.

IDEAS IN PRACTICE

Fuchsias in pots and baskets

Kathleen le Mare became a keen gardener when she moved to the country 15 years ago. Before that she didn't even like the feel of earth between her fingers. Hard to believe when you look at her garden and burgeoning greenhouse now.

The greenhouse measures 3.9m × 3.3m (13ft × 11ft) and in it she grows many plants but particularly fuchsias. She sells her plants at a once-a-year garden party and holds a small plant sale for the local Labour Party which always does well.

'I have always thought fuchsias to be absolutely exquisite. They are also easy to propagate. The only thing they lack is scent. They lend themselves to "designing"; you can train them into standards or pyramids, for instance. I joined the local fuchsia society and attended meetings and lectures for 12 months. There I met a grower who had some original ideas about growing and had written pamphlets which he sold at lectures. I thought his material was more interesting than anything I got out of the library.

'By joining a society you immediately get swaps as well. I did buy in a few of the varieties I couldn't locate quickly and I also took cuttings. I used to knock on people's door if I saw a fuchsia I liked and was seldom refused. They may not always know the variety but you can find out from a book because fuchsias are so individual. They are also comparatively late flowering here so the plants are often not in flower when I sell them. I keep a book with photographs of the varieties I grow and people love looking through it. Often they buy more than they originally intended.

'I now propagate all my own plants – about 60 varieties – from stock I have built up gradually.

'The way I sell is really for charity. The once-a-year garden party is in early summer when the fuchsias are at the right stage. If you are selling for charity you can always ask people to bring pots and trays.

'I also have a little trade selling them at the top of my basement steps. Also the gardener up the road puts in a request for fuchsias and pays me in kind with beans and produce from his garden.'

Recently Kathleen started to incorporate some of her fuchsias into hanging baskets which she hangs outside the house. Their opulence and grace moved her family and friends to ask for similar ones so she made some up and sold them. Now she has regular orders and keeps them 'ticking over' by buying twice as many baskets as she has customers and when the baskets are returned the following year she exchanges them immediately for others already planted up.

'The only reason I began with the baskets is that fuchsias absolutely ask for them. And they flower late enough in the season so that you can get them going without a heated greenhouse.' She uses fuchsias and lobelia and doesn't mix any further than that 'because if fuchsias are grown properly three or four will fill a basket. In garden centres you will often find baskets which include other plants with the fuchsias but they wouldn't need the others if they were patient at nipping the fuchsia buds to get a good bush.

'Plants should go straight into the basket when ready for potting on, if you have somewhere to hang the basket. They will establish much better that way. I feed them with general fertiliser until they are coming into bud and then use tomato fertiliser which encourages flowering and ripening. My baskets are best in early August (which is late for hanging baskets) because I pinch them back three or four times to achieve a mass of flowers.'

THE NITTY GRITTY

Training/ experience
If you are going to concentrate on only one type of plant you will need experience. Preparing hanging baskets and window boxes with mixed planting is easily learned. Join a society or club locally whose interest is the plant of your choice, or whose wider interest will include it. Go to lectures and meetings so that you can pick up information, cuttings, ideas, hints and enthusiasm.

Premises and equipment
If you are growing cuttings from your own plants and already own a greenhouse, you won't need much capital investment. And if you grow plants which can survive in an unheated greenhouse your running costs won't be very high either. You may need a small, low level heater just to keep the chill off the greenhouse in winter.

Compost, pots and containers are likely to be your biggest expense. It's worth looking in junk shops for unusual containers and shopping around for terracotta ones, which can vary in price. Check whether the ones you are interested in are frost proof. Many are not.

For hanging baskets you will need moss and polythene or foam to line the baskets. You will also need a large space such as a garage or outhouse in which to make up your containers or baskets and somewhere to hang the baskets and store the containers until they are sold.

Outlets
If your own window boxes, baskets and pot plants are spectacular you can start by selling to relatives and friends who will be keen to have something so fresh and pretty outside their homes. The big thing is to have a good show out-

side your own front door to impress people. You can move on to plant sales (in your own garden or plant society sales) or craft markets. Here you would be advised to concentrate on plants in pots rather than in baskets, though you could take one or two for show and take orders.

It is worth approaching banks, hotels, pubs and offices that have space for baskets, window boxes or tubs. Garden centres may buy planted containers and baskets from you to sell on.

Advertising and publicity

Advertising is not really necessary unless you are going into business on a large scale. Word of mouth should be all you need. Let it be known that you are prepared to make up a basket or propagate a particular plant for anyone who would like it. If you wanted to make more of a business out of it, put a notice up in a local shop or at the library.

How busy?

This depends on the scale of your operation, and does not have to be full time. You might have several days of potting up to do in advance of a sale or to complete an order. When not potting up you will have to spend some time propagating and tending plants.

What to charge

Ensure that your plants are in tip top condition and beautifully trained and use this as a selling point. Compare local produce and sell cheaper.

Plants for
offices

In recent years plants have become an essential part of the decor of a modern office. But most office workers do not have the time or the expertise to give the plants the care they need in large, centrally heated, air-conditioned spaces. A number of companies have now sprung up who provide and maintain large numbers of carefully chosen plants on a permanent basis. There is certainly a business opportunity here for someone who knows how to organise, position and maintain an indoor garden.

How to begin

It is possible to start on a modest scale, providing plants for small local offices. Architects, banks, building societies and solicitors all need to present a pleasant image to clients. Keep your customers to a minimum at first. Remember that you have to supply plants, pots, back-up and replacement plants. Until you are well established you could easily become overstretched if you take on too many clients.

To begin with you could probably manage with small premises, perhaps even working from your own garage. You will need some capital initially because both plants and containers are expensive and you need to acquire these before you can provide a scheme and get paid.

After the first six months to a year, you will need to have a stock of replacement plants so that you can take the first lot back for rehabilitation.

If you are supplying a small local business you might be able to grow and propagate suitable plants yourself, but the larger the commitment the less satisfactory this becomes, and for large contracts you should expect to buy in suitable plants and use your expertise to care for them.

Drawing up a business plan

You will need to draw up an initial agreement with each customer. They may want to rent the plants and containers from you or buy them outright and have a separate agreement for care and maintenance. You may be asked to work to a budget. Before you draw up an agreement, research the project thoroughly.

- Assess the premises carefully and decide which areas would benefit from plants. Bear in mind that the office is a working environment and the plants shouldn't interfere with personnel.
- Decide what sort of plants to provide, and check that their requirements match the office conditions.
- Itemise the types of plants and containers you would install, and their cost.
- Calculate the cost of travel to and from the premises for servicing the plants.
- If you have to employ someone to help with maintenance, watering or planting, include that cost.
- Also include the cost of compost and plant food.
- When working out what to charge, don't forget to incorporate a fee for yourself, based on your time plus a mark-up to cover overheads.

Matching plants to the environment

Many modern offices have an atrium or glass section running right up the building and this needs something spectacular in the way of foliage, either tall and slender trees standing at the bottom, or 'weeping' plants cascading down from above.

Dark corners need brightening up with plants that will survive in dark conditions. Modern low voltage lighting has tended to make offices darker and this is disastrous for some plants. Choose plants which don't mind gloomy conditions, such as *Aspidistra elatior* (see page 98).

Small offices or reception areas might like something compact such as a bottle garden or terrarium (see pages 101–3). Most offices will have a preference for foliage rather than colourful flowering plants – foliage is pleasing without being distracting and is often easier to look after.

If the customer does express a preference, make sure the chosen plants are suitable for the environment and suggest alternatives if not.

Maintenance This should include watering, cleaning, feeding, trimming, spraying and replacing plants as required.

Few offices offer ideal conditions for plants and they will soon suffer from lack of light or humidity or from having cigarettes stubbed out in their compost. When plants do become tired or air-conditioning-sick they should be exchanged for other healthier ones and given rehabilitation treatment.

Certain chemical sprays are not permitted in public places (like offices) unless you have a certificate from the Ministry of Agriculture, Fisheries and Food. Check with the Ministry before spraying.

Send your invoices for maintaining the plants in advance because businesses are notoriously slow in paying.

Containers There are a number of different varieties of pots to use: anything from ceramic, earthenware, aluminium, fibreglass or plastic to lined baskets – but unless you are working on a very small scale and can visit frequently, all should be self watering (see page 76).

The containers should be suitable for the shape and size of plant and, if necessary, stand on a bed of pebbles to retain moisture.

Some suitable foliage plants for offices

- *Aspidistra elatior* (cast iron plant) has strap-like leaves. Will grow in fairly dim light and average room temperature. Water regularly but less in winter. Repot every five years in spring. Divide plants in spring or summer.
- *Chamaerops excelsa* (European fan palm). Grows up to 2m (6ft) high with fan shaped fronds. Needs plenty of light and normal room temperature. Likes lots of water. Soil-based compost. Propagate from fresh seed in early spring or from basal suckers.
- *Cordyline* and *Dracaena* (false palms). There are three which are particularly easy to grow: *C. australis*, *D. marginata* and *D. draco*. Will tolerate light shade and a warm atmosphere. Water regularly so compost is always moist and mist leaves regularly. Repot every two years in spring. Propagate by removing crown from old, leggy plant and re-planting in potting compost with bottom heat, or by cane cuttings: cut the bare trunk into several pieces and insert each in seed and cutting compost, either

horizontally or planted upright (if upright make sure you bury the end which was lower when it was growing).

- *Dieffenbachia seguine* (dumb cane). There are several types. Will reach 2m (6ft). Likes partial shade in summer, bright light in winter. Average room temperature, but not below 15°C (60°F) in winter. Water regularly during growing season. Mist frequently or surround pot with damp peat. Repot annually in spring. Propagate by potting up top crown or use pieces of stem as cane cuttings (see above). Some varieties produce offshoots which can be used as cuttings.

- *Davallia canariensis* (hare's foot fern). Good for hanging baskets or shallow containers. Most forms are tolerant of dry air. Likes fairly good light and average to warm room temperatures. Water moderately and let top of compost dry before watering again. Propagate by rhizome cuttings.

- × *Fatshedera* (tree ivy). Has large, shiny, five-lobed leaves. Needs support. Medium light or by shady window. Prefers cool position but will survive in heated room if kept humid. Place pot on moist pebble tray. Water moderately. Use soil-based compost. Repot well-established plants each year. Plant very firmly. Propagate by tip cuttings or air layering.

- *Fatsia japonica* (false castor oil plant). A quick growing shrub with large glossy leaves. Plenty of light but will accept sunless window. Adaptable to most temperatures. Water plentifully during growing season. Use rich soil-based compost with more than average balanced fertiliser. Propagate by stem cuttings, tip cuttings or from seed.

- *Ferns* like medium light or bright filtered light but will withstand a poorly lit corner for a few weeks at a time. Normal room temperature. Water generously. Use half-strength fertiliser, rich in nitrogen to encourage lush growth. Grow in rich organic compost. Propagate by division of the rhizome for *adiantums* and *polystichums*, or tip cuttings of the rhizomes or runners. Baby-making ferns like *Asplenium bulbiferum* (mother fern) can be propagated from the bulbils.

- *Ficus*. There are several suitable varieties including: *F. buxifolia*, quick growing shrub with thin arching stems, and copper coloured bark; *F. elastica* (rubber plant), large, shiny leaves off central stem; *F. lyrata* (fiddle-back fig), large violin-shaped leaves. Medium light. Can be acclimatised to wide range of temperatures. Water whenever top half of compost becomes dry. Pot in smallish pots in spring (*ficus* like to be cramped). Propagation is by tip cuttings or air layering but is difficult and slow and best done by professionals.

- *Grevillea robusta* (silk oak). Fast growing evergreen tree, can reach 2m (6ft). Will grow in medium light but likes direct sunlight. In winter must be in a light position. Tolerant of wide range of temperatures but must have humidity.

- *Hedera helix* (ivy). Many ivies are suitable for indoor growing and provide a green base for innumerable planting schemes. They do need bright light and variegated forms should have two or three hours of sun every day. Will tolerate a wide range of room temperatures. Provide extra humidity in high temperatures. Water moderately in the growing period. Use soil-based compost. Propagate by cuttings or layering.

- *Howeia* (Kentia palm). Dark green arching fronds can grow to 2.5m (8ft). Bright or medium light, normal to warm room temperature. Water generously during growth period. Use soil-based potting compost. Repot once a year. Propagate by fresh seed (may take six years).

- *Livistona australis* (Australian fan palm). Dark green leaves on slender stalks. *L. chinensis* (Chinese fan) has bright green leaves. Bright filtered light – no direct sun. Normal room temperatures. Water moderately. If the room is warm enough they need no rest period. Repot into soil-based compost. Propagate from fresh seed (takes several years).

- *Monstera deliciosa* (Swiss cheese plant). Has attractive deeply incised leaves. Can grow to 5.5m (18ft). Bright, filtered light (will tolerate direct sun in winter). Normal room temperatures. Water sparingly but keep humid. Use soil-based compost. Difficult to propagate: tip cuttings, air layering and seed are all possible.

- *Nephrolepis cordifolia* (sword fern) and *N. exaltata* (Boston fern). Both have feathery arching foliage. Bright light without direct sun. Will tolerate medium light for four to five weeks. Normal room temperatures. Water regularly and thoroughly. Use peat-based compost. Propagate from plantlets or spores.

- *Philodendron*. Various good plants, all have large shapely glossy green leaves. Bright filtered light, no direct sun. Normal room temperatures, moderate watering. Soil-based compost. Repot when necessary. Propagate climbing varieties by stem cuttings, root cuttings, tip cuttings. Non-climbers should be grown from fresh seed. Climbing plants should be given a moist structure they can cling to with their aerial roots, e.g. moss tied round a stake and sprayed regularly.

- *Sansevieria* (mother-in-law's tongue) includes *S. cylindrica, S. trifasciata, S. liberica*, tall plants with lance-shaped leaves. Plenty of bright sunlight, very warm conditions. Moderate water. Use soil-based compost with a third of coarse sand or perlite added. Doesn't mind being cramped in the pot. Propagate by leaf cuttings or division.

Terrariums and bottle gardens

These are self-contained more or less self-perpetuating miniature gardens in which water is drawn up from the compost, delivers nutrients to the plant and then goes out through the leaves, down the sides of the plant and back into the compost. They are a good way of providing a miniature garden for people living or working in very dry atmospheres.

Containers for terrariums and bottle gardens
You can make a mini garden in all sorts of glass containers from thoroughly cleaned chemical carboys to large sweet jars, kitchen storage jars, aquariums or specially constructed 'stained glass' terrariums. A terrarium has a lid which lifts off and is generally easier to plant and maintain than a bottle.

The container must be absolutely clean. Wash it out with detergent at least three times, rinsing thoroughly between washes. Don't use very hot water for washing glass or it may break.

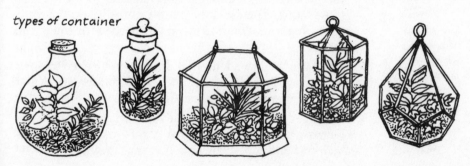

types of container

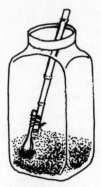

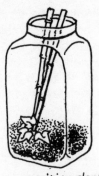

dig hole with spoon

position plant

manoeuvre roots with fork

firm the compost

Planting a terrarium or bottle garden

improvised tools

cotton reel

join pieces of plywood with tape

Put a layer of pebbles or gravel in the bottom with a broken up charcoal stick which will prevent the compost becoming sour.

- Add a loam- or peat-based compost. John Innes potting compost No. 2 with some added peat and grit is good. A 5cm (2in) layer should be enough for a kitchen storage jar but 15cm (6in) is needed for a large carboy. Pour the compost through a funnel for a bottle garden.

- Planting a bottle garden can be tricky and improvised implements are needed. Use two lengths of wooden dowel or bamboo cane with a spoon attached to one and a fork to the other.

- Wrap each plant in stiff paper to protect it as it goes through the bottle neck. Dig the hole with the spoon, manoeuvre the roots into place with the fork, cover them with soil and firm down. A cork or cotton reel attached to the dowel is good for firming down the compost. A pair of tweezers made from two flat pieces of plywood will help to position any pieces of ornamental stone.

- When the planting is complete, mist the foliage and water the compost and leave for ten days to make sure it is just moist. Then seal the jar or put the lid on the terrarium. No more watering should be needed for four to six weeks.

- A pin attached to a length of dowel can be used to spear and remove any plant litter and a razor blade can be used for trimming plants if necessary.

- Feeding is unnecessary and only encourages the plants to outgrow the container. When plants grow too big, lift them out and replace with something smaller.

- Never place a bottle garden or terrarium in direct sunlight.

Suitable plants for a bottle garden

Use only foliage plants in containers with narrow necks or you will have difficulty getting out decayed flower heads.

Choose slow growing plants which won't fill the container too quickly: *Cryptanthus acaulis* (bromeliad) 'Green earth star', 7.5cm (3in); 7.5cm (3in); *Cryptanthus fosterianus*, 15cm (6in); *Cryptanthus roseo-pictus*, 7.5cm (3in); *Hedera helix* (ivy) 'Little Eva', 'Ivalace', 'Glacier', 'Jubilee', trailing plants; *Peperomia hederaefolia*, 15cm (6in); *Sansevieria* 'Hahnii' (mother-in-law's tongue), 15cm (6in).

Suitable plants for a terrarium

In addition to the above plants you could add: *Saintpaulia* (African violet), 12cm (5in); *Saxifraga*, 10cm (4in); *Begonia boweri*, 23cm (9in); *Aphelandra squarrosa* 'Louisaie', 13cm (9in); and other small plants with flowers.

IDEAS IN PRACTICE

A growing concern

Ed Wolf lives in an indoor garden. His house is filled with tall palms and green foliage, leading through a glass conservatory-like wall to the greenery of his garden. He is a professional operator and supplies plants to large London companies.

Ed trained in Holland where plant technology is very much in advance of most other countries. He first worked in an English nursery and then for a company which supplied plants to London offices. 'In those days that meant one large container in the entrance hall or a pot in the board room where people poured their excess gin on to the African violets.'

He set up on his own 13 years ago 'with a watering can', not with the idea of creating a business but just to pay the bills. Now he finds he is one of the ten biggest companies in London. Initially he operated from two double garages but now he has 180 sq m (2,000 sq ft) and wonders how he managed without.

'Our main strength is in offering a good service. Our plants are good looking, healthy, suitable for their situation and nobody has to phone me a second time. I always deal with queries straight away.

'I was lucky in that, after working in the city, I knew exactly where to go for work and I brought in a £3,000 job on the first day, plus £2,500 in maintenance including replacements.

'I started with just a few customers, and then grew with them. Basically I am a small-thinking man. My aim has always been to stay small. I don't advertise and I don't have our address or phone number on the van. All our growth is by word of mouth. My main aim is to look inwards at existing customers and grow with them. We don't sell plants, we sell service.'

Ed discourages discussion with his clients. 'All I expect them to do is enjoy the plants and pay the bills, nothing else. When they realise that you know what you are doing they usually leave you to get on with it.'

THE NITTY GRITTY

Training/ experience

Ed Wolf considers there are two enormously important factors: you must be 100 per cent sure of what you are doing and you need a large measure of luck (though you can help luck to happen by being enthusiastic, aware and efficient). Obviously it is going to help enormously if you have worked in a similar company with a good training scheme.

There are a few courses; nurseries will tell you how to grow and good flower shops will provide experience.

Premises and equipment

You will need a light, airy space to store plants during reha- bilitation. Your own home, a heated greenhouse or warm, adequately lit garage or shed are all suitable.

You will also need plenty of containers (preferably self watering (see page 76), watering cans, indoor plant food, compost, pesticides etc and transport.

The containers and the plants themselves will be fairly expensive and you will need to find the money for those before sending a bill to your client so there may be quite a substantial initial expense. If you begin with just one client, providing plants for reception and office areas, and build up business slowly, this should not be crippling. If you can pro- pagate your own plants, that will of course be a tremendous saving.

Outlets

You only need a few small contracts or one big one to begin with. Approach offices which have an eye for the environ- ment either because they are in the environment business (architects, designers) or because they have to impress clients (solicitors, estate agents, banks, building societies, shops).

Gift shops and flower shops may be interested in taking bottle gardens and terrariums.

Advertising and publicity

Distribute leaflets or business cards, or write on business-headed paper to local offices. Once you have a few satisfied customers, word of mouth will be all you need.

How busy?

Depending on how confident you are and how much capital you want to raise, a contract may involve providing two or three plants for a small office or plants throughout the whole of a large office building. If you build your business up to the scale of Ed Wolf's you will be busy all day with phone calls, plant problems, managing staff, and replacing pots and plants.

What to charge

Do a bit of sleuthing and find out from florists whether they provide an office service or find out from friends in offices with good indoor planting what they pay for it.

3
GARDENING
SERVICES

Gardening
for others

Gardening for others is a growing area. Over 80 per cent of the population own their own homes but are too busy working full time to pay off the mortgage to spend time on their gardens. They are, however, house and garden proud and do need help. Or they may be elderly and unable to do the bending and lifting. Such people need a conscientious gardener and there is a real gap to be filled. If you have had some experience and know the basic needs of different plants and how to provide them you could be kept very busy. Many people who advertise themselves as gardeners don't actually know the difference between the noxious dock and the edible sorrel and will dig up a precious bed of herbs without realising what they have done – which means that a *good* gardener will always be in demand.

Gardening is something that can be done on an entirely 'friendly' or barter basis: you look after someone's garden and they let you take home most of the produce and pick the flowers, for instance. Or it can be treated as a part-time job in which you undertake to maintain, weed, water or mow once or twice a week. Or it can be treated as a serious earning job which will take up a full week's working time.

One problem for the serious but unqualified gardener is knowing what to charge. Because there are many retired people who do gardening just to top up pensions, many employers fail to see it as a serious job and are inclined to underpay. This undercuts the wage a full-time gardener needs to make a respectable living. However, if you are knowledgeable and have 'green fingers' you may persuade garden owners to pay a living wage. Once established in an area, particularly a fairly affluent one, you should find plenty of gardens which need attention.

Some gardening services to offer

There are many garden owners who enjoy gardening but would like someone to come in and do specific jobs for them. Most of these are jobs that need either strength or a special skill, or both. Even digging, which may sound like a simple thing to do, can be done badly.

Clearing

This is a useful ability. In some cases it just needs brute strength and a sickle or a tough mechanical mower or cutter; in others a knowledge of what to pull up and what to leave (ie a knowledge of plants). Meadows or large spaces can be cleared with a scythe.

Good clearing should include cleaning up afterwards and burning rubbish or putting it on the compost heap. Make sure the instructions you have been given are understood and you don't clear more than is intended.

In autumn there is always a demand for people to clear fallen leaves.

Weeding

This is one of the least enjoyable gardening jobs, and hence a good service to offer.

Digging

Many people actually enjoy digging but find it too hard on the back, or simply have not got time for it.

Mowing lawns

Lawns should be mowed every week in spring and summer and every two weeks in autumn. Many people are prepared to pay someone to cut the grass. It helps if you have an understanding of machinery.

Pruning

Many people are unsure about pruning. They don't know when, where or how much to cut. Someone with experience and knowledge could make this a speciality.

Trimming and shaping hedges

This is often a difficult and time-consuming job and one that many gardeners would prefer to pay someone else to do.

Propagating

This is mainly a spring occupation though it can carry on through the summer. Sowing from seed, and pricking out, growing from cuttings and layering are all very useful skills for a gardener. But you do need experience.

Planting and moving plants

This is autumn and spring work, though container-grown plants can be planted at most times of year unless it is very hot or very cold.

Structural work

This is good winter work, much of which can be done when the rest of the garden is dormant. All the following are useful skills but they need strength and stamina:

- building walls
- laying flagstones
- building steps
- putting up fences
- building rock gardens

IDEAS IN PRACTICE

Learning as you go

Philip Glynn decided to become a gardener at the age of 28. He had spent some years as a telephone engineer and picture framer, while at the same time growing organic vegetables for himself and his family.

He found he had an aptitude for gardening and started getting work locally, which led to his being offered a three-day-a-week job maintaining a large, recently designed garden in a village. As time went by he was offered work in other gardens and is now making a satisfactory living and even turning jobs away. His natural instinct for the plants, his genuine interest – supplemented by a great deal of reading – and his day-to-day experience have turned him into a capable and knowledgeable gardener.

IDEAS IN PRACTICE

Making the most of experience

Toni Willis is an enterprising woman in her sixties who looks a great deal younger than her age. She is a creative person who used to make costumes for the Royal Opera and has always been a keen amateur gardener.

'When my marriage came to an end I decided to do what I have always loved doing – gardening.

'At the time I was feeling very low and someone rang me

and said "Would you like to do some gardening?" I went trailing up to a gloomy looking house where I found the owner bending over a flower pot. "My God, you're a woman," he said, "I don't suppose you'll be any good, but you can try."

'At about the same time I began to maintain the shared garden of a group of studios rented to architects. They don't want to pay for more than one day's work a week so I just keep it as lawn surrounded by shrubs, which don't need much maintenance.'

From those beginnings she, too, is now having to turn people away. Her clients have all come to her by word of mouth, mainly through her previous work. They are all people who have little time for gardening but appreciate their gardens and her skills.

Toni insists that she is not a garden planner. 'I don't plan formally. In my opinion a garden should be planned as you work on it. Many clients want the garden to look very good straight away and you have to shove plants in like crazy – too close together and in the wrong places. They always look horrible in the long run. I much prefer to put plants in gradually as I learn about the garden, and what the soil is like, where the sun shines at what time of day and so on. So I do quite a lot of planning, but only informally and off the cuff.

'I have taken on out-of-work boys to move rocks around, but normally I do all that sort of thing myself. Gardening is a lovely thing to do but you have to be strong and have a good back!'

THE NITTY GRITTY

Training/ experience   It is not necessary to have formal training to become a good and efficient gardener but it is essential to be deeply interested and to have experience. Special training helps you to acquire particular skills and knowledge in a disciplined way and consequently can save much time, unnecessary labour – and costly mistakes. Short courses on pruning, propagation, etc. can be helpful. There are many books and magazines on all aspects of gardening.

Premises and equipment   You don't need premises of your own if you are gardening for other people.

Equipment and items like string and stakes should be provided by the client. But some clients may need to be enlightened about what tools are necessary. Many gardeners prefer to use their own tools (for example lawn mower, strimmer, spade and fork, secateurs), which they find well balanced and the right size, and which they know have been properly maintained.

You will need some form of transport for carrying your own tools, and for carrying bags of peat, compost etc.

Outlets

If you live in a rural area with many large gardens, there should be no shortage of clients. Elderly people often need a gardener to take on the most strenuous work, such as tree and hedge trimming and digging. Owners of weekend cottages may be glad of someone who can keep the garden under control during the week and mow the lawn ready for the weekend. Owners of town houses are usually glad to have a gardener they can trust, and the 'gentrified' areas offer excellent opportunities for experienced gardeners or gardeners with a speciality.

Large business premises are often fronted by a garden area. They will be keen to keep it looking tidy as its appearance will reflect on the company's image.

Advertising and publicity

You can either become attached to one important garden and through this achieve a reputation, which will bring you other clients, or you can distribute leaflets or your card through letterboxes and hope to get several gardens to divide your time and energies between. It is always a good idea to offer references and keep photographic records of the gardens you have worked in so that you can show them to potential clients.

If you want to specialise in hedge clipping, lawn mowing or clearing, then you could try local leafletting (markets, car parks), or, again, by popping your card through letterboxes. A small advertisement in the classified section of the local paper may be useful, or cards in local shop windows.

How busy?

Gardeners can find themselves working seven days a week, if they want to. However, hours are often flexible and it is possible to take the odd day off, specially in a slack season, or to take on work to suit yourself. Spring and autumn are the busiest seasons, with planting and replanting, cutting back, pruning, feeding, mulching and so on. Summer and winter should be less busy.

What to charge

Charges for gardening can vary enormously. Some big nurseries charge the highest amount, but this is no guarantee that clients will get a better or more experienced gardener.

As a guide, an inexperienced jobbing gardener might charge the equivalent of a cleaning woman or a window cleaner, but a good 'creative' gardener, who takes a large amount of responsibility for plants and layout in general, should be able to charge very much more. Check up on the various charges locally. Those who care for their gardens should be prepared to pay respectable rates to get good service.

Garden
planning

In the days of Capability Brown and Humphry Repton garden planning and landscaping was the province of the very large estate. But modern garden planning is just as relevant to small gardens, so the opportunities for garden planning are tremendous.

The emphasis nowadays is on gardens that will not need much maintenance. A planner may prefer to maintain the garden for a year after planting, to see whether the plants like their positions and whether there need be any changes made. After that the garden will probably look after itself to a large extent, for today's gardens can be a mixture of paving, shrubs and herbaceous plants which will deter weeds and provide interesting foliage throughout the year.

Possible types of planning required

A garden planner may be expected to do all or any of the following:

- Position a greenhouse.
- Make suggestions for conservatories or summer houses and perhaps point the way to an architect or company who could design and build one.
- Design herbaceous beds, rock gardens, alpine gardens, kitchen gardens and herb gardens.
- Site and design hedges and screens.
- Advise on and possibly locate fountains, statuary, patio pots and garden furniture.
- Provide planting plans which may be for problem areas such as an area overshadowed by trees.
- Design a colour scheme.

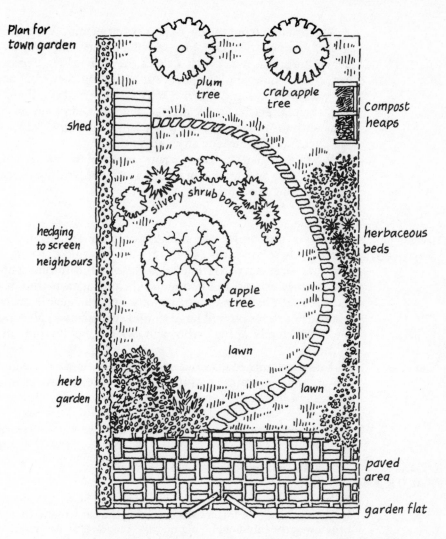

Plan for town garden

plum tree

crab apple tree

Compost heaps

shed

silvery shrub border

hedging to screen neighbours

herbaceous beds

apple tree

lawn

lawn

herb garden

paved area

garden flat

It is the planner's job to purchase the plants and do the planting, or to organise any or all of the above tasks, through sub-contractors and other specialists.

Client briefing and agreements

Your relationship with the client is important and you must make sure they understand exactly what you intend. Some will require a very detailed plan, others may be pleased, when they know your work, to let you get on with it.

Some form of agreement should always be given in writing between the parties concerned. This doesn't need to be very elaborate but should state what work has been agreed on, the time it should take, what is to be paid for it and when payment is to be made.

The briefing from the client is very important. Some time should be spent discussing the client's wishes and the planner should come away with a check list of the client's priorities – for example play space, sun lounging corner, space for washing lines and rubbish bins, ornamental pond etc.

If the planner has a good brief there should be no problems with the customer changing plans. If this does happen the client should pay for any extra time.

When they use sub-contractors, many planners arrange for the client and sub-contractor to make their own agreement for the work they do.

Sub-contractors

When you are under pressure to complete an assignment quickly, there are services of every kind to make use of. It may be necessary to find a number of different sub-contractors to work on one job. Contractors who are excellent at paving may not be very knowledgeable about plants. For that you will have to find specialists in planting and 'soft landscaping' who will do all the buying and planting.

Knowing how to get hold of such people is part of a garden planner's training and there are trade associations through whom they can be contacted.

IDEAS IN PRACTICE

'A design and build' practice

Jude Moraes runs her own garden 'design and build' practice. In planner's jargon, this means designing the garden and then organising the building, laying out and planting, as described above. About ten years ago she says she 'got the self-sufficiency bug', and considered going to live in the country and working a few acres. 'I wanted to grow the country's food – organically, of course'. She decided it would be impossible to embark on such a project without some training and did a year's full-time course in commercial horticulture on a government retraining grant at a college of agriculture and horticulture. She had never taken an exam before in her life.

Jude then put one two-line advertisement in the local paper (the only one she's ever needed), and took her bike and her secateurs to various local gardening jobs.

'But I found it very lonely working on my own; I needed someone to bounce ideas off. As luck would have it I met a girl on a part-time ecology course who had the same basic points of view and we've been working together ever since.'

Most of their work is on private gardens but they will undertake anything from giving advice, to planning, installing and maintaining a garden. Or the client can take over once the garden is completed. They usually maintain a garden for the first year. 'We don't necessarily do a complete garden all at once. Some owners can't afford to have it done in one fell swoop. It makes sense anyway to do things by degrees. You have to think and structure. It's probably not until about the third year that a new client may begin to realise what you have done for them.

'We do not grow our own plants. I do have a space in my own garden where plants can "rest" while waiting to go to their final abodes but we do not "grow" plants at all. We get our plants from about 35 different nurseries. You can, of course, get plants cheaper by buying just a few varieties in hundreds from a garden centre, but that's not what we want; we prefer to offer variety.'

Jude and her partner have worked for local councils and even created a three acre garden and saved it from being built on. That was funded by the local tenants' association with the local council and the government.

Other public sites have included a windy, bleak garden on a council estate intended as a place for the residents to sit. Usually such gardens won't be maintained by the council afterwards so they planted big trees as a screen – 'Well, they will be big!'

'I do think it's a good idea to work for someone else for a bit to learn through their mistakes rather than your own. And do things by degrees.'

IDEAS IN PRACTICE

Part-time planning

Sheila Stedman gave up work when her children were young, but she had always been keen on gardening and as the children reached school age she wondered how to use that interest. She didn't feel like starting a full blown landscape architecture course, which lasts five years, so instead went on a one year's one-day-a-week course on garden planning.

When the course was complete, she found that work came her way simply by word of mouth and she has not had to advertise at all.

'I have planned a number of gardens near my home, I suppose about 20 in all. I'm working on quite a challenging project at the moment, a garden whose owners are going away for three years and want to find a 'mature' garden by the time they come back. That's not as easy as it sounds, because the plants must be able to cope while the owners are away, and establish themselves without much watering and so on in that time. This sort of work is interesting because you get all sorts of different gardens and clients who want different layouts and environments.'

Sheila can design and draw up a complete garden plan, including landscaping and organising the building and the planting out, or she can design a simple colour theme or create a garden which will be particularly interesting at certain times of year, such as a winter garden or a spring garden. Although she would be willing to go back after a few months to re-assess the planting, she would not expect to pop back to a garden several times a week to water plants while the owners were away.

'Ideally I would like to work just mornings or perhaps two full days a week. I don't work in the holidays and I have a weak back which means that long periods spent over the drawing board can be trying. I always get contractors in for carting stone because I couldn't possibly do any lifting myself. In fact, I don't do any of the physical work and that's another good thing about a planning training. You learn how to find people to do the physical work for you.'

As a planner, she feels involved with her gardens and is always willing to go back after a year and make suggestions for changes. However she finds that there is a real difficulty in charging a fee for that kind of after care. 'It can be dreadfully difficult. Quite a few people I work for are friends and I feel very diffident about asking them for a fee. On the other hand I really don't feel I should be expected to put in valuable time just for a gin and tonic.

'I have found it can be a good idea to "swap" clients with other people in the planning business, so I take their friends as clients and they take mine. Then there's no embarrassment about money and the relationship can be on a professional level.'

THE NITTY GRITTY

Training/ experience Some professional training is essential before you set up in business. There are garden planning courses for beginners and more advanced courses which give thorough grounding in the techniques and practicalities of garden design and how to approach it professionally.

It is important to visit gardens, read books, talk to other gardeners and generally keep alive your interest and awareness of what's possible, what's traditional, what's new and changes in fashion.

Courses on practical horticulture may include design as part of the curriculum and, although they may not be so thorough, it would be possible to start in a small way from such a course. One of the most important things a course can offer is the contacts you make while there. The more people you know in the horticultural world, the more you have to call on when specialist skills or sub-contracting work are needed.

Premises and equipment

You will not need special premises. Perhaps (as in Jude Moraes' case) you will want space in which to keep plants for a while before putting them into the gardens. Though if you are getting plants through a contractor who does the planting too, you will not even need that.

A good drawing board and ergonomically designed chair and drawing materials and a long tape measure are essential.

You will need all the reference material you can lay your hands on: books, magazines, catalogues, addresses, specialists, photographs and notebooks.

Because you need so little in the way of premises and equipment, the capital expenses are not great. The biggest expense is likely to be at the moment of buying stock and materials for a new garden, so you will almost certainly need a small capital sum to start up. Ask for an advance from your client or borrow from your bank.

Outlets

Keep an eye open for new housing developments in your area. The developers themselves and the new home-owners are both possible outlets. Owners of existing gardens may want to make changes, and hotels with large gardens are another possibility.

Advertising and publicity

When starting, either advertise or get written up in the local paper, or drop your card through local letterboxes (especially in areas where houses are changing hands and new owners may be looking to plan the garden afresh).

Get to know the local gardening firms and garden centres. It's possible they might find work for you, or at least display your card or pass on your name.

Keep photographic records of the gardens you have designed to show as examples of your work.

How busy? Garden planning can be anything from offering intermittent advice to friends to setting up business with a team of workers. Most people who go into garden planning very much enjoy grappling with the problems and challenges set by different gardens and different clients and find themselves working pretty well full time.

What to charge Charging is very difficult because each garden varies so enormously in size and scope. A large garden on several levels may take six hours to survey whereas a small town garden might take only an hour, so the costing is bound to be fairly arbitrary. The most sensible basis seems to be to charge so much an hour and try to be realistic about the time a survey and drawing will take.

If you are setting out on your own, find out what local garden planners are charging and fall into line with them. Work out your costs and what you think you should earn in an hour, say, or a day, and add them up. You can charge by the hour or you can cost a job and charge a straight fee. If there's a good deal of structural work involved, relate your prices to what the local builder charges.

Much careful working out of planting schemes and the advantages of your contacts in the trade and your own administrative abilities are all worth a serious fee to the garden owner. Even if your clients know a bit about gardening, they would not be coming to you if they felt confident or had time to do the garden on their own, so do not undercharge. If using sub-contractors, make sure you are aware of their charges and add a mark-up.

On top of all this there will be charges for any plants, pots, compost etc. that you buy. For these the planner buys at trade price and sells to the client at retail price and that is possibly where most of the profit comes from.

4
OFFSHOOTS

Flower
arranging

Flower arranging is a highly professional and skilled art. Many people begin by working on church flowers and that is probably the best way to acquire the basic skills. An experienced flower arranger will know where and when to buy or pick the best flowers, how to make sure they last a long time and will have a very sophisticated sense of colour and form.

There are good opportunities for making money from flower arranging. You could offer a variety of arrangements, from tiny posies, corsages and nosegays to big formal arrangements for weddings, christenings, large parties or the hallways of stately homes. Hotels and restaurants might use your services, and anyone running a flower shop might also want help to arrange flowers for special occasions.

Flower arranging is a skilful craft and the quickest way to learn is through a local flower arranging society. There you will pick up knowledge and acquire the techniques of cutting, watering, supporting and making the flowers last.

You may want to develop a particular style. The western tradition of abundant, colourful, scented and symmetrical arrangements has its counterpart in the Japanese Ikebana tradition of sparse, sculptural arrangements. Different styles may be required for weddings, posies and bouquets.

Other ideas for flower arrangers

There is scope for imaginative packaging of flowers.
- Flowers prettily arranged in small baskets give much more pleasure than 'just another bunch'.
- Bunches of flowers which are colour co-ordinated have a special appeal and can fetch quite high prices.

- Table decorations for restaurants are always in demand.
- Large striking room decorations for hotels, stately homes or office reception areas is a possible area to specialise in.
- If you become knowledgeable about flower arranging you can make quite a good business out of supplying cuttings or plants which are either not available or very expensive at garden centres. You may find a market for these at your local flower arranging club.
- Posies and nosegays are often made with sweet smelling flowers and herbs. They are carried by bridesmaids, used as table decorations, make pretty birthday presents, or can be given to friends. There are many opportunities here for invention and initiative. Make them to order, either direct from yourself or through a local flower shop.

Conditioning flowers
Keeping flowers fresh is part of the flower arranger's skill and stock in trade. Freshness depends on the flowers being picked early in the morning and being conditioned according to type. This could involve crushing the stems or filling hollow stems with water and sealing (see page 82). They must then be dealt with quickly and deftly. While arranging the flowers keep them in a cool place and avoid damaging the flower heads.

Hints for flower arrangers
Fill the vase three-quarters full of water before arranging flowers. This adds to the weight so the vase is unlikely to topple over. When the arrangement is completed, fill the vase to the top.

- It is not necessary to change the water every day, but fresh water must be added daily to keep up the water level. A tiny drop of mild disinfectant or proprietary preservative will keep it fresh.
- Foul water shortens the life of flowers. The vase should be emptied and refilled as soon as the water begins to go green. Glass vases are not ideal containers as they let in sunlight and this causes bacterial activity.
- Wilting flowers can often be revived by re-cutting the stems under water and dipping the end in boiling water.

Containers Use your imagination in the use of containers. You will get all sorts of marvellous results from breaking away from the usual vase shapes. Try using:

- glass storage jars, including shop sweet jars
- baskets of all shapes and sizes (which can be lined)
- jugs, including antique or second-hand washstand jugs
- bowls, large and small
- tea caddies and other tins
- terracotta urns, window boxes and plants
- cache pots
- copper and brass goblets and pans

Lining a container
Baskets, cracked ceramics and some other containers will need lining before you fill them with water. The best thing is to find a plastic bowl which will fit into the container but remain hidden inside. Or you can use a lining of kitchen foil for small containers or a double lining of thick foil for larger ones.

Keeping flowers and bouquets fresh

- Flowers which are going to be worn or carried should be prepared very shortly before they are needed because they will quickly wilt. Give them a long drink of water before arranging them.
- Some flowers can be prepared up to 12 hours in advance if they are kept in a cool place (but not the fridge, which is too cold). These include Peruvian lilies (*Alstroemeria*), stephanotis, gypsophila and barely open roses.
- Sweet peas, open roses, hellebores and lilies-of-the-valley are short lived and should be prepared as near to the event as possible.
- Flowers which have been prepared should be kept in sealed polythene bags (not too restricting) to retain their moisture.
- Keep bouquets out of full sun, away from heat (radiators and fires), off the television and away from very strong lamps.
- Carnations do not like being placed near fruit.
- You can spray flower arrangements with water at night to keep them fresh or cover them with damp muslin.

Mimosa heads should be sprayed several times a day to keep the flower heads fluffy.

- Do not spray flowers which are to be pressed later for posterity because they may become discoloured. Instead seal them in polythene bags to retain moisture.
- Hydrangea heads absorb water so before arranging soak them for a few minutes in cool water.

Plants for the flower arranger's garden

All the following last well in water. Some have a long flowering season. The plants have been grouped together according to the season when their flowers first appear.

Spring flowers

Artemisia abrotanum (southernwood or lad's love): several varieties with feathery, silvery foliage. Crush stems, dip ends in boiling water and stand in water before arranging.

Bergenia (elephant's ears): heavy spikes of pink flowers, fleshy leaves. Stand in deep water before arranging.

Cheiranthus (wallflower): biennial. Wide range of colours, lovely smell. Crush stems and stand in water.

Convallaria (lily-of-the-valley): little white bells in spring. Stand in water before arranging. Useful for posies.

Euphorbia (spurge): yellow, green, sometimes red heads. Staunch sap with a naked flame. Stand in water.

Ferns: many forms from strap-like to lacy. Holds ends of stalks over match or candle flame to seal. Stand in water before arranging.

Narcissus: yellow, white, pheasant's eye, single or in clusters. Cut while in bud. Stand in water before arranging.

Polemonium (Jacob's ladder): spikes of white or blue flowers with very pretty deeply cut leaves. Stand in water before arranging.

Primula: lots of bright colours. Primroses, polyanthus, cowslips etc. Good for posies. Stand in water before arranging.

Ruta graveolens (rue): prettily shaped blue-grey leaves, grown for foliage rather than flowers. Pungent smell. Crush stems and stand in water before arranging.

Summer and autumn flowers

Acanthus (bear's breeches): tall spikes of purple/white hooded flowers and glossy green leaves. Dip stems in boiling water before arranging.

Achillea: large plate-like yellow (or pink or red) flowers. Crunch stems.

Aconitum (monk's hood): tall, deep, inky-blue spikes of hooded flowers. Also pale blue, white, cream. Stand in water before arranging.

Agapanthus: large, round balls of blue flowers. Stand in water before arranging.

Alstroemeria (Peruvian lily): trumpets of good pinks and reds on long stems. Stand in water before arranging.

Aster: tall daisy flowers, many cultivars in bright colours. Crush stems then stand in water before arranging.

Astilbe: feathery pointed brushes of pinks, reds and whites on long stems. Stand in water before arranging.

Calendula (marigold): hardy annual. Bright orange. Stand in water before arranging.

Ceanothus (Californian lilac): shrub of small powder blue flowers. Crush stems. Stand in water before arranging.

Clarkia: annual, bright colours in pinks and purples. Dip stems in boiling water.

Dianthus (carnation, garden pink, sweet william): white, pink and red flowers. Stand in water before arranging.

Echinops ritro (globe thistle): spikey globe flowers about the size of ping pong balls in silvery blue. Stand in water before arranging.

Eryngium (sea holly): spiky bluish and blue/silver plants. Stand in water before arranging.

Gypsophila (baby's breath): tiny white flowers in profusion. Stand in water before arranging.

Lathyrus (everlasting pea, sweet pea): large pea flowers in May in wonderful pastel and dark colours. Some fragrant. Stand in water before arranging.

Lilium (lilies): colourful waxy trumpets on long stems. Stand in water before arranging.

Phlox: many flowered heads of bright colours on tall stalks. Crush stems and stand in water before arranging.

Polygonum bistorta (snakeweed): ground cover foliage and pink spikes on straight stems which are still decorative when they have gone brown. Dip stems in boiling water then stand in water before arranging. Good for posies.

Rudbeckia (cone flower): daisy-like flowers in interesting colours. Dip stems in boiling water and stand in water before arranging.

Scabiosa caucasica (scabious): mauve, purple, white or primrose yellow pincushion flowers. Stand in water before arranging.

Senecio cineraria (sea ragwort): yellow daisy-like flowers with silvery foliage. Crush stems and stand in water before arranging.

Solidago canadensis (golden rod): egg yolk-yellow flowers in large plumes. Crush stems and stand in water before arranging.

Stachys lanata (lamb's ears): soft furry grey leaves. Stand in water before arranging.

Winter flowers

Cornus (dogwood): range of shrubs grown for their bright red, orange or yellow bark in winter. Crush stems.

Helleborus niger (Christmas rose): whitish pink saucer-shaped flowers. Prick stems with pin behind flower head and stand in water before arranging.

Helleborus corsicus (Corsican hellebore): greeny yellow flowers in umbels on tall fat stems. Prick stems with a pin behind flower head and stand in water before arranging.

Iris (reticulata group): blue or yellow flowers on short stems. Stand in water before arranging. Remove dead flowers as they occur.

IDEAS IN PRACTICE

A paying hobby

Patsy Brown is a teacher but has been interested in flower arranging for many years. Her speciality is in large 'country' arrangements suitable for large homes, and church flowers. She grows a spectacular variety of herbaceous plants in the garden which she and her husband created eight years ago.

Patsy's skills were acquired through her local flower club and she was eventually 'pushed' into becoming a demonstrator and examiner. 'I have taught many people to do church flowers when they came as helpers, and although church flowers on their own would hardly be a money-making concern, churches are immensely helpful as places to practise.

'The more practice you can get the better. I know of a man

who learned his craft from the more experienced arrangers in church and now he is doing very well on his own, providing simple and beautiful funeral arrangements. He charges very reasonable prices but he makes quite a good profit.'

Social contact is one of the best ways of finding work when you first start, says Patsy. 'During the conversation it may turn out that someone wants flowers for a wedding or a party, then you can offer to do them. That's a good way to begin. And you can be very competitive in your prices. If a big company charges so much for an arrangement there's no reason why you should not do an equally good or better one for half that price.

'In my garden I grow a lot of unusual plants. I have a catmint that is useful in arrangements because it is darker and more compact than the normal one. I have a herbaceous form of phlomis, which has a prettier pale yellow flower than the normal egg yolk one. I also grow many different varieties of sage and a compact low growing golden rod. Hostas are marvellous for arranging and I grow a variety of those too. All of these would be excellent in flower arrangements and for dividing and selling as small plants in pots at club meetings.

'Other possible outlets are local hotels and caterers who organise local weddings. You may not earn a lot of money but there is likely to be a constant stream of work.'

Patsy thinks that florists are not very imaginative in Britain. 'What they offer is often disappointing. It's quite different in America where they are full of new ideas (but everything costs a fortune). I am sure there must be a market for something more unusual and distinctive in the way of flowers, than is normally on offer.'

IDEAS IN PRACTICE	**Wedding bouquets**

Beryl Bird specialises in bridal bouquets and headdresses. 'In the early days I did a lot of charity work and then my husband retired and my daughter suggested I should make a business out of the flowers.

'Wedding bouquets demand perfect flowers, so I get them from New Covent Garden flower market in London or my ex-teacher's flower shop. For other arrangements I get cheap but beautifully fresh flowers from the local market.

'I often do all the flowers for a wedding, including headdresses, bouquets and flowers for the church and top table. I always try to do the arranging in the cool of the early morning or evening.

'I give the bride plenty of time to consider what colour she wants. Most people want roses whatever the season, and I also use white lilies just as they are opening – but not too many –

and wired Singapore orchids. I also use freesias and spray carnations and, if I can't get lilies, I buy stephanotis but it has to be wired so is quite tricky to use. These flowers are all good with white or peach dresses. If someone is wearing a peacock blue dress, say, I shall try to find a flower to pick up the colour. I like to use ferns. Maidenhair fern looks lovely with long trails of ribbons and satin.'

THE NITTY GRITTY

Training/ experience

If you are going to have anything to do with arranging flowers professionally you must have lessons. Joining a local flower club is probably the best way to learn. At a club you can watch other people and pick up techniques and inspiration. You will also learn which are the best flowers and foliage to grow in your garden for arranging. Through a club you may be encouraged to become a demonstrator, which is good experience. There may also be opportunities to buy plants and accessories cheaply.

Premises and equipment

A utility room would be useful but any place where there is a sink and room to work will do.

You will need various shapes and sizes of vases, bowls, jugs and other containers, and shelves to store them on. You will also need dry foam, chicken wire, string, rose wire, gutta-percha tape (for binding round wired stems), adhesive clay, florists' spikes, funnels, ribbons, sharp knives, secateurs, florists' scissors and wire cutters.

You can buy baskets at reasonable prices through wholesalers but flower arranging clubs can order them for you cheaply, which is a great advantage. Local markets often have a good selection of cheap and interesting baskets too.

When looking for flowers, remember that people with allotments may be happy to let you have some of the flowers they grow.

Outlets

In some cases, churches may pay a small fee to have a special flower arrangement done for a wedding, christening or funeral. Otherwise the family organising the event will pay.

But the best outlet may be caterers who want flower arrangements for weddings and other occasions – they usually have good contacts with florists and funeral directors.

Make contact with churches, hotels, restaurants, caterers and flower shops and watch out for opportunities when local weddings, funerals, christenings and birthday parties crop up in conversation. Work from specific orders, rather than completing arrangements and then trying to find buyers. With fresh flowers that's really too much of a gamble.

Advertising and publicity

Advertising in flower arranging magazines might bring some response. For bridal bouquets and arrangements try advertising in local papers and brides' magazines.

Take photographs of as much of your work as possible so that you can show prospective clients your style and capabilities.

How busy?

This is another of the enviable hobbies in which you can be as busy as you choose unless you make a long term commitment to a particular client who may want arrangements at awkward times such as weekends.

What to charge

Check with the local flower club and with what's charged generally in your area and charge to suit the circumstances. Your charges will partly depend on the flowers used since some are much more expensive than others. If clients want flowers out of season your prices will shoot up.

Take into account travel expenses (you may have to travel some distance to get the flowers you want, and to deliver them), any assistants you hire, containers, equipment, ribbons and your time.

Dried
flowers

Dried flowers have a timeless appeal. Bunches of 'everlasting' flowers are sold in gift shops; dried love-in-a-mist and lavender are scattered artlessly in practically every magazine photograph of a farmhouse kitchen or country interior, heaped in baskets in Victorian room sets and arranged in vases in elegant hallways.

There is something enchanting about dried flowers and leaves which have been carefully processed and retained their colour. Even those which have faded and become papery have an appeal. Dried grasses we can admire in autumn and summer along the hedgerows but many other plants lend themselves to drying just as well. In fact, most plants can be dried. Beech and other leaves, teasels and docks can all be incorporated effectively in large, stately arrangements. Smaller dried flowers are attractive arranged in baskets, vases or other containers and have the advantage of needing no further maintenance apart from dusting! Flower heads that have been dried separately can be used in arrangements with other flowers by fixing the heads to wires.

Many people grow their own flowers for drying; others have no garden or feel that growing is a different skill altogether or takes up too much time and prefer to buy fresh flowers and then dry them.

Because dried flowers are so popular there are many possible ways of marketing them. They can be sold as bunches for the customer to create something with, or as completed 'arrangements'.

Some money-making ideas

- Arrange flowers in pretty baskets; colour schemes and inventiveness are very important.
- Sell in bundles of separate varieties and colours, but prettily put together so the customer wants to buy more than one.
- Sell in different containers, matching flowers to container: copper vessels, ceramic mugs and jugs, old cauldrons, soup tureens, dolls' prams. Collect in jumble sales, junk shops and markets for future use.
- Sell heads of 'everlasting' flowers piled into a pretty bowl or basket.
- Sell small flower heads separately in tinted glass jars.
- Sell baskets filled up with large petals from pansies to roses, removed from their stems.
- Sell dried flower posies wrapped in doilies.
- Sell arrangements to match particular decors for people moving house or decorating.
- Sell dried flower posies to local museums, gift shops, craft shops.
- Dry flowers from the gardens of people who would like a memento.
- Sell pot pourris in little bowls or baskets with a tiny 'topping up' bottle of essential oil.
- Sell winter garlands made out of fir cones and nuts (see page 135).
- Make and sell miniature collages (see page 139).

Drying flowers and foliage

There are four established drying techniques: hanging flowers upside down to dry in a warm, dry place; standing the stems in glycerine which is the most suitable treatment for foliage such as beech leaves; laying them in silica gel (or alum or borax for the more delicate flowers) which is expensive but can be used many times over or covering them in sand, which is a 'cheap and cheerful' method, effective for more robust flower and grass heads.

There is also the relatively new technique of drying in a microwave oven. Several people are experimenting with this and quite exciting things can be done, such as drying large, open roses.

Hanging flowers to dry naturally

This is the easiest way to preserve stemmed flowers. Simply tie them together in bunches and suspend upside down from hooks on the ceiling in a warm, dry, airy place.

Flowers to dry by hanging
Achillea, pick when flowers are fully open.

Aster novi-belgii (Michaelmas daisies), pick in autumn.

Clarkia, pick all summer.

Helichrysum (everlasting or straw flowers), pick when just open.

Helipterum, cut before the petals are fully expanded.

Hydrangea, cut when flowers are fully open.

Limonium (sea lavender or statice), pick when flowers are fully open.

Nigella (love-in-a-mist), pick as flowers open.

Papaver (poppies), select buds just showing colour and scald the stems immediately to seal the ends.

Polygonum, pick all summer.

Ranunculus, pick all summer.

Drying flowers with sand

Beach sand is a cheaper alternative to silica gel and can be used for practising on flower heads. It is suitable for drying heavier flower heads.

1 Put 2.5cm (1in) sand in the bottom of a box.

2 Place the flower heads on top and cover with another layer of sand.

3 Put the box in the airing cupboard and leave for about 7 days.

Flowers to dry in sand
Dahlias, pick in summer when newly open.

Helleborus corsicus, *H. foetidus*, *H. altrorubens* (hellebores), pick in early spring when just open and *H. niger* (Christmas rose) in winter.

Peonies, pick in spring/early summer before too far open.

Tulips, pick in spring when newly open.

Zinnias, pick in summer when newly open.

Drying with alum, borax or silica gel

wire through flower head

airtight tin

when dry slip corn stalk over wire or attach to twig

Silica gel is expensive but can be re-used, as can alum and borax. Dry out in a warm oven.

1 Remove the stems from the flower heads and cut a length of narrow wire. Make a tiny hook at one end. Push the straight end of the wire through the flower face.

2 Cover the bottom of an airtight tin with 6mm (¼in) drying agent. Place the flowers in the tin and put the lid on.

3 When the flower has dried you can slip a corn stalk over the wire or attach it to a twig.

Flowers to dry in alum or borax

Alum and borax are good for delicate flowers but too fine for heavier blossoms.

Calendula (marigold), pick from early summer, when just open.

Clematis, pick when newly opened.

Myosotis (forget-me-not), pick from spring to early summer.

Narcissus, pick while flowers are only just open in early spring.

Nigella (love-in-a-mist), pick as flowers open.

Primula, pick while flowers are still unblemished.

Rosebuds, pick when not too tightly in bud.

Scilla, pick in spring when newly open.

Flowers to dry in silica gel

Silica gel is good for small and delicate flowers and flower heads such as:

primroses, violets, forget-me-nots, snowdrops, periwinkles, wood anemones, gypsophila.

Preserving in glycerine

This is a good method for branches, twigs and foliage. Pick them in summer when they are still fresh-looking with the sap rising as this is when they take up the glycerine best.

1 Use 1 part glycerine to 2 parts hot water. Put the mixture into a tall, narrow jug, vase or jar which will allow the liquid to come 10–13cm (4–5in) up the stem.

2 Stand the stems in this and leave in a dry dimmish place until a slight sweat appears on the surface.

Plants to preserve in glycerine

Fagus (beech), pick when leaves are still young and fresh.

Fatsia japonica (false castor oil plant), pick in spring when leaves are still young.

Ferns, pick when growth is still fresh and young.

Hedera (ivies), pick when leaves are still fresh and tender.

Rhododendrons, pick in spring when flowers are only just open.

Some hints on preserving

- Pick when flowers are in their prime. If there is pollen on the stamens, the flowers should dry well.
- Dry flower heads in shoe boxes in the airing cupboard.
- Keep grasses green by putting their heads in sand.
- If by any chance the flower heads have dried unsatisfactorily, don't waste them, they can be put into a pot pourri.
- A hint of metallic car spray paint on dried hydrangea heads (the same colour as the flower) – just on one side, helps to seal them and highlights their colour.
- Many people protect their flowers from sunlight, but dampness is much more likely to draw colour from a flower, so always store in a dry place.
- Store preserved flowers and foliage in boxes to protect from dust. Use an anti-moth preparation. They should survive for years like this.

Instructions for making a winter garland

Garlands made out of fir cones and nuts are long lasting and attractive and popular. They are time consuming to make, but cheap as the ingredients are lying around on the ground. They make good centrepieces for dinner tables in winter and specially at Christmas. Although attractive in their natural colours they could be painted or sprayed.

You will need larch fir cones, elderberries, tree fungi, lichens, mosses and nuts. You can use a woven straw base, generally available from florists. Cover it with crêpe paper. Trim the branches and leaves and staple into place with heavy duty staples. Fill any spaces with lichen and moss.

A more permanent garland can be made by gluing the ingredients on to a platter or large plate. Use all kinds of fir cones and different nuts and other hard coated fruits in browns and reds.

Instructions for making pot pourris

Pot pourris are always popular, but shop bought ones vary enormously in quality and are expensive. There are innumerable possible variations, depending on the proportions of the particular flowers and herbs or spices used, and the essential oils.

When making a pot pourri, add the most delicate petals last of all so they won't get bruised. Suitable ingredients include naturally dried garden flowers such as roses, lilac, lavender, carnations, lilies-of-the-valley, violas, wallflowers, in fact most scented flowers and aromatic herbs as well as scented fruits, dried rinds of oranges, lemons, limes and tangerines. You can add brightly coloured petals which have no scent, just for looks. Wormwood (*Artemisia absinthium*) makes a good, cheap base for a herbal pot pourri.

You also need essential oils and fixatives such as gum benzoin or equal quantities of cinnamon and orris root to hold the scent of the oils.

Here is a simple basic recipe:

1½ tsps ground cinnamon	6 drops rose oil
1½ tsps orris root	2 drops lavender oil
4 or 5 cloves	about 4 cups dried petals,
½oz powdered allspice	leaves and rinds
One small drop of	1oz cinnamon stick,
patchouli oil	broken up

Mix the powdered spices and cloves in a bowl. Add the oils and mix well. Gently add the dried ingredients and cinnamon stick making sure everything is thoroughly mixed. Put into a sealed jar, shake well and leave for a week or ten days.

Pot pourris will last a long time if topped up with fixatives and oils from time to time. You can also add more petals and leaves from the garden.

Experiment with different mixtures of leaves and flowers

and different essential oils. Sell in jars or in sealed plastic bags which in turn may be put in decorative pots, ready to unseal.

IDEAS IN
PRACTICE

Growing and drying

Janie Phillips is married to a farmer and has three small children so is not ready to go into full-time business. But she does manage to grow and dry flowers which she sells 'sporadically'. She specialises in arrangements to match a client's colour scheme.

At the back of the house is a fine herbaceous bed and behind that a small 'allotment' where she grows flowers in rows for drying. These include statice, clarkia, 'Bells of Ireland' (*Molucella laevis*) and *Helipterum humboldtianum* from Australia – a pretty, daisy-like 'everlasting' flower. Half-hardy annuals are sown in the greenhouse then planted in the beds as soon as possible. She has a three month season of cutting and drying.

Rows of drying bunches hang from the beams in her kitchen and in a small room up the back stairs. In an outside shed she dries grasses. 'I keep the secateurs permanently in the car, in case something interesting catches my eye,' she says.

'Larkspur has to be dried quickly and goes above the Aga. Cornflowers dried in the bottom oven were not successful – too hot perhaps. I have bunches of love-in-a-mist which I spray silver for Christmas. I've dried a few peonies but I'm not sure if they've been successful and I've also dried lavender, which I absolutely love, and delphiniums. Hydrangeas come from our holiday cottage. You flick them and if they sound papery they're ready. Just about anything will dry if you pick it at the right stage.'

'People who are moving house will bring me a snippet of wallpaper and I can do an arrangement to match. I've done a lot of posies as well. In fact, I sold 50 to the local natural history museum this year.'

THE NITTY GRITTY

Training/
experience

It's not necessary to have any formal training to dry flowers. There are plenty of books on the subject, and it is quite a simple process. However, you will need practice, as different flowers require different drying techniques and time.

If you are going to sell dried flower arrangements rather than bunches, join a flower arranging club to get some practical advice and experience.

Premises and equipment

For drying stemmed flowers you will need a shed or garage, a large kitchen or an old stable where you can hang them. It should be dry, warm and preferably dark. Dryness is more important than temperature and heat on its own without an extractor doesn't always work when the weather's cold and damp. A de-humidifier will help to remove moisture.

If you are drying flower heads, you will not need so much space. A large airing cupboard will do for the actual drying.

Equipment itself is minimal: beach sand, alum, borax, silica gel and/or glycerine; long boxes for storing dried, stemmed flowers; wires and twigs or straw to make the stems of flower heads.

If turning your flowers into pictures you will need a chest of drawers to keep them in while waiting to use them. Small cardboard boxes with transparent lids make it easy to identify what's inside the box.

For arrangements, you will need something to use as a base: baskets, bowls, boxes or whatever catches your eye.

Outlets

You can sell from home at occasional selling parties (see page 157) or by advertising in the local paper. Christmas is a good time to do this when people are looking for gift ideas.

Craft fairs, markets, gift shops and flower shops are all likely outlets. Mail order is also a possibility. Interior designers, hotels and restaurants are worth approaching.

Advertising and publicity

Drying flowers is a popular craft and you will probably be competing with others in your area. Advertisements or a write-up in a local paper will help. For a small-scale, part-time business, word of mouth by friends will probably be sufficient.

How busy?

There are many different stages to creating dried flowers, from preparing the ground and growing the plants, to collecting and drying them. How busy you are will depend on the scale of your operation.

What to charge

Weigh up the time and effort you put into the business and the cost of materials and reckon how much you want or need to break even or make a profit. Compare prices of other people's similar work and don't go too much out of key with them (unless you think they are wildly under or over pricing).

Pressed flower pictures

Pressed flower pictures and greeting cards have a wide appeal and are usually expensive, reflecting the time and skill that have gone into making them. If you are artistic and imaginative you should be able to make money from pressing flowers and using them in attractive ways.

Pressing flowers is a relatively simple process that is easily learned and doesn't require much space or capital.

There are opportunities to make money even if you don't have a garden or it is too small, such as pressing flowers for friends or turning wedding bouquets into pictures to make a lasting memento of the day.

Money-making ideas

- Make pictures from the flowers out of the gardens of people who are moving house. Use their favourite flowers and foliage to create, for example, a scene representing part of the garden.

- Christening pictures make unusual presents. Make collages with petals, using blue for a boy and pink for a girl, or spell out the child's name using flowers.

- Make plant calendars with a different picture for each month, using seasonal flowers and leaves – for example, a page of primulas, snowdrops, ivy, hellebore, catkins, skeleton leaves for a winter month and a page of buttercups, cranesbills, roses, cow parsley, ladies' bedstraw and daisies for an early summer month.

- Make greetings cards, labels and bookmarks from tiny flowers or petals. Keep the composition simple. Interesting card for the backing can be found in specialist stationers or art suppliers.

- Make unusual pictures from dried herbs and berries for an alternative to still-life oil paintings to hang in the kitchen.
- Decorate wooden mirror or picture frames by glueing pressed flowers and leaves on to the corners. The whole frame should be given several coats of varnish after this treatment. Use very thin pressed flowers and leaves. This technique can be applied to small boxes as well.
- Decorated candles, especially white ones, make charming presents. When the candles are lit the flowers seem to glow and look even prettier. The technique is to hold a pressed flower on to the candle and brush melted wax over it in a very thin layer.
- Pressed flowers can transform simple cardboard photograph frames.

Hints on pressing flowers

- Press the flowers as soon as you can after picking.
- Build up layers of absorbent tissue or blotting paper, lay the plant material carefully on this, cover with another layer of tissue and then layers of newspaper. Put this into the press.
- Keep flowers and leaves of a similar thickness together.
- Get as many items as possible on each sheet, but without them touching each other.
- The quicker the material dries the brighter the colours, so put the presses in an airing cupboard or warm room.
- Telephone directories or encyclopaedias make alternative presses.
- For the first three or four days, exchange the damp newspaper every day with dry newspaper. Be careful not to disturb the flowers in their tissue. After that change it every two days or so.
- Store the finished flowers still in their tissue paper, with corrugated paper sheets placed between every ten pressed sheets to allow air to circulate.

Pressing a wedding bouquet

Making a pressed flower picture from a wedding bouquet offers good scope for the imagination. You will only be able to make a small picture from a small bouquet but a large one will allow you to make a border from the smaller petals and leaves to frame the picture. You could even incorporate some fabric from the bride's wedding dress or veil.

The first thing to do when you receive the bouquet for pressing is revive the flowers, which may have wilted during the day. Separate them gently, put them in a polythene bag and leave them in the fridge for an hour or two. Start pressing as soon as possible so that the flowers keep as much of their colour as possible.

Colour-coded flowers and foliage

Reds: paeonies, fuchsias, old roses, pink cow parsley, pink cranesbill, dianthus, astilbe, potentilla, polygonum, red chrysanthemum, Japanese anemone, 'De Caen' anemone, geum, red clover, sorrel, hydrangea, pieris 'mountain fire' leaves.

Blues: larkspur, primula, blue cranesbill, periwinkle (*Vinca*), bluebells, hyacinths, bugle (*Ajuga*), forget-me-not, viola, delphinium, ceanothus, blue anemones.

Yellows and greens: ranunculus, primulas (cowslips, primroses), lichens, ferns and mosses, grasses, ivies, strawberry leaves, astrantia, chamomile, chrysanthemum.

White and silver: chrysanthemum, gypsophila, achillea, snowdrops, skeleton leaves, honesty, philadelphus, lilac, cow parsley, lichens, stachys leaves, white clematis and its seed heads, white roses, wood anemones.

IDEAS IN PRACTICE

Pictures from wedding bouquets

Susan Ganney was all set to go into floristry and had enrolled at a local horticultural college, when her back began to give her trouble and she was told it would be a long term problem. She cancelled the course. However, she didn't like the idea of sitting around doing nothing and she still wanted to work with flowers so she decided to make pressed flower cards from the flowers in her garden, and taught herself how to do it.

'I've always "had a way" with flowers and this is a sedentary means of getting pleasure from them,' she says. She makes framed pictures using a great number of different flowers, mostly grouped by colour and she specialises in preserving wedding bouquets.

Recently she advertised for the first time in a magazine for brides and the response was overwhelming. From that advertisement she received many orders for pressing wedding bouquets and turning them into pictures.

'Most of my work is through a brides' magazine at present but I have got customers, particularly in my local area, who come back and ask for more pictures.'

'I really like making big pictures. I'd love to do people's gardens – go to their gardens, pick their flowers and do a big picture. That sort of thing is difficult to publicise though, because it's unusual and hard to explain.

'My business is so small and different that I get interesting things to do because the people who come to me are individualists. I was recently asked to dry 21 red roses and turn them into a picture of a rose bowl. This year I went to one of the big craft fairs where several people saw my work and this week I'm doing a design for someone I met there.'

She sells a few of her pictures through a local shop which sells dried flowers. Susan thinks she may have to employ someone to help with the wedding flowers. 'I want to keep the business small but I wouldn't mind getting other people to do the day-to-day preparation of the flowers so long as I keep control of the design side and personal service.'

'My sister grows montbretia (*Crocosomia × crocosmiiflora*) in her garden and presses it for me. In fact I bully several friends with large herbaceous borders to press flowers for me.

'I find pricing very difficult. People say I don't charge enough, while I think it sounds a lot, but I certainly don't make much money. The work is labour intensive but I'm happy that I can earn a little money doing what I love doing.

THE NITTY GRITTY

Training/ experience

It is possible to teach yourself to press flowers and make pictures out of them but it will help if you go to classes or join a club. Watching and talking to other people will give you ideas for new colour flower and leaf combinations, as well as different uses for your pressed flowers. The more individual and confident your designs are, the more likely you will be to find customers.

Premises and equipment

You can press flowers in a one-roomed apartment if you don't mind perching presses on every shelf. A fair number of presses can be kept in a large cupboard or a spare bedroom without disrupting the rest of the household. An airing cupboard is best as it is dry and warm. It is also a good place to store the dried material until you are ready to use it. Otherwise you will need some sort of chest or drawer space for storing the pressed flowers. Small cardboard boxes with transparent lids make it easy to see what's inside each box.

You will need a table or desk to work at.

If you are sitting down for long periods, get yourself a typist's chair with an adjustable height mechanism which will be more supportive than a dining chair. Or try one of the 'kneeling' chairs which are specially designed to make the back support itself instead of allowing you to slouch.

Ready made presses are not expensive and the traditional method of using the family encyclopaedia (or telephone directories) works very well for light pressing. You will, however, still need absorbent tissue paper or blotting paper, newspaper and corrugated paper.

For pictures you will need tweezers, adhesive, card, paper, backing card and frames.

Outlets

Craft and gift shops and craft fairs are obvious outlets for pressed flower pictures. The local library might exhibit your work. If you live near a stately home which is open to the public they might take your goods, as examples of local craft work, to sell in their shop.

Stalls at local markets, car boot sales, 'environment days' at horticultural colleges and agricultural fairs can all be worthwhile if you have the time to attend them. Check the venue out first for suitability.

More enterprising florists, particularly those specialising in dried flowers, may be happy to take pictures to hang in the shop on a sale or return basis.

Advertising and publicity

As Susan Ganney found, one advertisement in the right magazine can be worth any amount of advertising in the wrong one. A bridal magazine was obviously a good choice for someone willing to make something out of wedding bouquets. Magazines which appeal to home owners, or garden lovers might also produce a good response.

How busy?

One of the good things about pressing flowers is that, theoretically, you can be as busy or as idle as you please. That is, until you start advertising. Then you will begin to find you have commitments and deadlines. However, the work is very much in your own time and it should be possible to arrange things to suit you.

What to charge

If you are lucky enough to belong to a club which has worked out pricing guidelines, do make use of them. If not, go round local shops and check the quality and prices of corresponding work.

Tea

gardens

Many people who sell plants find it worth their while to diversify – especially when relying on passing trade. Those who have a big enough garden might not only grow unusual plants to sell but also put on their stall vegetables or home made jams and preserves. If you live in a 'holiday' area it can make sense to open up your garden and offer teas.

Selling teas is an easy and enjoyable thing to do, and a well-run teas business may make as much or more money than the garden itself, and will help to bring in customers. It calls for a fair amount of energy, time and talent. You must be naturally gregarious and enthusiastic not just about gardening but also about cooking and receiving visitors. You also need a supportive family who won't mind people wandering about in their garden and who may even be prepared to help.

If you begin on a small scale you won't need much capital; you probably have sufficient garden furniture, table cloths and china to cater for a few customers at a time.

Presentation There is more to providing a good tea than the food and the garden; people greatly appreciate the way in which it is served. If you are making do with an old table, cover it with an attractive cotton print, or gingham cloth and choose pretty china which will do credit to the food. Put a small jug of home grown flowers on the table. If there is no shade to sit in, provide umbrellas on hot sunny days – your guests will be more comfortable and the umbrellas will provide a holiday atmosphere.

What to serve

Unless you are happy for people to come in and only order a drink, offer set teas only. These could be traditional cream teas, sandwich teas or cake teas.

Baked foods such as cakes and breads store well in the freezer so it is possible to prepare large quantities in advance and thaw as required. Your repertoire could include the following: scones, tea breads, flapjacks and tray bakes, large cakes and buns, biscuits, sandwiches and homemade preserves (see page 147).

IDEAS IN PRACTICE

Teas on the lawn

Eight years ago Wendy Gunn and her husband spent a holiday in the country, found a 300-year-old house with a large field and within ten days had sold their town house and moved in. More or less single handed, Wendy has turned the field into a garden. She grows fruit, vegetables and flowers and sells them and home made jams from a stall at the bottom of the garden. In addition to this she sells teas on the lawn.

A flower garden borders the path to the tea area and is a random planting of individual delights, rather like an old-fashioned patchwork quilt. This is an attraction to visitors and keeps people occupied if they have to wait for a table.

'I've become much more interested in gardening than I expected,' says Wendy. 'I have joined The Hardy Plant Society, The Cottage Garden Society, several propagation schemes and I spend a lot of money on seed. I read and read and read – books, magazines, anything to do with plants and food. It wouldn't bother me at all if I didn't have a television.'

Wendy makes scones, cakes, biscuits and jams for the teas and she serves them to her customers herself. She's an outgoing person and enjoys meeting people and chatting about her garden. Because she lives off the beaten track the teas are a pleasant interruption to her obsession with the plants and don't take up too much of her time as people tend to come only on fine weekends.

The only publicity for the teas is a blackboard at the roadside. 'We might do a leaflet next year. But we don't want too many visitors' she says.

THE NITTY GRITTY

Training/ experience

You need to be an energetic and keen gardener and cook, and enjoy meeting and dealing with people. You also need to be very disciplined.

It is important to be aware of the regulations concerning food and also those concerning using your home to run a business from, so check these with the local authority.

Premises and equipment

If you plan to invite visitors into your domain, you will need large enough premises with attractive flowerbeds and an area suitable for serving teas not too far from the kitchen. You will need to have a toilet for visitors to use supplied with running water, soap and towels. You will also need tea services, tables and seating. A freezer will be useful. See also 'Refreshments' on page 162.

Outlets

Your own garden is the outlet.

Advertising and publicity

Provided you are in a pleasant country area, where people pass who are on holiday or retired or have free time for other reasons, a blackboard by the roadside, where it can easily be seen should bring in plenty of passing trade (see page 160). Once people have visited and enjoyed your garden and the food, they will probably come back. They will also tell their friends and trade can build up quite quickly. To attract a few more people you might try 'leafletting' the car park in your nearest town or putting a tiny advertisement in a local newspaper.

How busy?

You can choose how busy you are by choosing when to open and what to serve. If you are offering teas as a way to attract customers into your garden in the hope that they will buy plants and produce, then the garden itself and making preserves will keep you busy the rest of the time.

What to charge

Work out the basic cost of each item, add something for your time and to cover overheads, plus a small percentage for profit. See what others are charging for teas locally and compare quality, portions and prices.

Preserves

If you grow fruit, vegetables and herbs, an obvious way of making money is to turn them into jams, jellies, pickles and other preserves. Provided you make sure you conform to the various labelling and weights and measures regulations, (see page 162), it can be a satisfying way of making money.

It is often possible to sell through local markets and enterprising local shops. Delicatessens, craft shops, gift shops and tea rooms all exist, which are prepared to sell tasty and attractively packaged preserves.

As with so many 'selling' projects, it always helps if you can make your product different (and, of course, better) than any competition and thus more appealing.

Some ideas for foods to sell

Jams and jellies
Try unusual fruits such as quince, mulberry, rowanberry or grape; unusual combinations of fruits such as greengage and apple, gooseberry and elderflower, strawberry and redcurrant; or spicy and peppery fruit jellies to eat with meats such as redcurrant and pepper, spiced redcurrant, apple and green peppercorns.

Fruit curds and cheeses
You need large quantities of fruit for these so make them when there is a glut. Curds could be: blackberry and apple curd, gooseberry and ginger curd, apricot and lemon curd, spiced apple butter, marrow and lemon curd, plum cheese.

Fruits in alcohol
Preserving fruit in alcohol is expensive but makes good Christmas presents. You could try apricots or raspberries in brandy, peaches in *eau de vie*, pears in port wine.

Chutneys and pickles

Make these good and spicy and interesting such as hot lime and peach chutney; peach, pumpkin and tomato chutney; pear chutney; beetroot chutney; and pickled pears.

Sauces

Possibilities are chilli tomato sauce, lemon sauce with dill, mint sauce, horseradish sauce, herby mustard sauce.

Salad dressings

Vary these depending on what herbs you have available. Horseradish dressing, herby olive oil and lemon dressing, herb mayonnaise, sweet and sour dressing with fresh ginger, garlic dressing.

Vinegars

You can use herbs and fruit in vinegars. Raspberry vinegar, strawberry vinegar, apple vinegar, dill vinegar, thyme vinegar, tarragon vinegar.

Oils

Try olive oil flavoured with rosemary, tarragon or thyme.

Composition of food

Any foods you are planning to sell such as jams, preserves and tomato sauce must conform to certain standards of composition laid down by law. You must check (with the Ministry of Agriculture, Fisheries and Food in the UK) to see whether there is any legislation covering the foods you are planning to make.

Ideas for presentation and packaging

People are more likely to buy a product if it is attractively packaged and labelled. It is always a good idea to suggest uses on the labels of more unusual products.

- Very simple glass jam pots with screw-on lids look attractive, provide they have pretty labels. You can follow the French example and give the jars gingham covers over the screw tops, held in place with elastic bands or ribbons.
- Preserving jars with screw-on or snap-on lids and a rubber seal look attractive.
- Vinegars should be sold in plain glass bottles so that you can see the colour and any herbs, such as tarragon, floating inside. Use pretty labels.

- Two or four small jars of different flavoured jams and jellies packaged together in one basket make good presents.

- You can sell your products in ceramic pots which will put the price up but could be a 'special' purchase at Christmas.

- Small, jam pot sized own-label carrier bags can be sold to hold the jams, especially for people buying them as presents.

- Make up special seasonal gift packs. Combine your home-made herby mustard with the local delicatessen's honey-smoked ham at Christmas, for example. Or package two types of jam together and sell as a 'breakfast gift'.

Labelling

There are regulations governing labelling as well as the composition of food. Check these out before you start.

- The name of the food must be precise enough to inform the buyer of its exact nature: not just 'Mint Delight' but 'Mint Delight Jelly'.

- The ingredients must be listed and the list must be headed by the word 'ingredients'. They must be in descending order of weight. Any regulations will give guidelines on how to list ingredients.

- Jam labels must state the sugar content (e.g. 'total sugar content 65g per 100g'), and the sugar content determines what the product can be called – ranging from 'jams' to 'extra jams' and 'jellies'.

- The name and address of the maker must be on the label, sufficiently detailed for the postal system to find it.

- If the food will not keep for 18 months or more, the minimum durability must be indicated on the label.

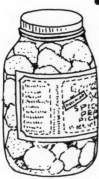

Ingredients:
Pears,
sugar,
cider vinegar,
onions,
sultanas,
mustard,
nutmeg
cloves,
salt,
allspice

Orchard House
Little Ashley, Northants

Garden Treats

homemade

SPICED
PEAR
PICKLE

net wt 170g   6oz

- All the information must be easy to read and easy to understand and visible on or through the packaging.

IDEAS IN PRACTICE

Home preserving

Sue Gillies makes mustards, jams, herbal jellies, herbal vinegars and herbal oils. She sells through five local shops and occasional craft fairs. In December she fills Christmas hampers with her own preserves together with wine and smoked salmon. She sells these through local shops or at open days in her home.

She has compiled an address list of customers and potential customers, including names obtained through her husband's business, and informs them of new products she is selling locally or of her next selling party. 'This year I'm going to produce a brochure – if I have time. When you are doing everything yourself, researching, buying, making, selling and packing, time is at a premium.'

Her first venture into selling was when she saw an interesting looking recipe for a mustard. She made a batch and sold them to her local greengrocer. 'It was totally illegal; there are all sorts of rules, regulations and restrictions on selling food including the sizes of the jars and what's on the labels (see page 162). It's a minefield.

'When I designed the label I asked the local health inspector to look at it. He'd never come across anything like it before and was as lost as I was. Apparently there's a completely different set of rules for sweet and savoury products.'

'I was green in other ways too. I didn't know where to get jam jars but I did know where to get honey jars so I used those, and that turned out to be illegal.'

'I can't afford to have different labels printed for each flavour, so I just have the basic label printed and write in the details by hand in any quiet moment.'

Sue has an upstairs storeroom and a small work room where she packs herbs and spices, but there are jars stacked up in every available corner of the house. There are problems dealing with large quantities, for example the sheer weight of a box containing several jars of preserves. Sue's husband helps set up the stalls when she goes to fairs and carries the boxes for her.

Sue grows fresh herbs for her jellies in the back garden, but she requires larger quantities of herbs for the vinegars and oils and so cultivates another herb garden in part of her father's kitchen garden.

Soon she will have to face the dilemma of whether to expand or not. Expansion would mean finding a small industrial unit and perhaps committing herself to employing a helper.

THE NITTY GRITTY

Training/ experience

As far as the products are concerned, it helps if you have had experience making preserves and have worked out reliable recipes before you begin.

You don't need formal training to get weights and measures and labelling regulations right, but you must seek advice from the weights and measures department of your local authority. It is a complicated business, particularly for sweet preserves. Vinegars, pickles and other savoury items pose less of a problem.

Premises and equipment

You can run quite a thriving little business from a very tiny kitchen. You will certainly need at least one room or garage space which you can set aside for jars and bottles and the boxes to carry them in, and for labels, leaflets and other paraphernalia.

It is often quite difficult to track down suppliers of glass jars of the correct sizes. Look in the telephone directory and trade magazines. It can be difficult to get manufacturers to sell you small quantities, but persevere; some are more accommodating than others.

You will also need a refractometer to check the sugar content of preserves, in addition to large pans, scales and ordinary kitchen equipment; see also 'Food legislation' page 163.

Outlets

Try local delicatessens, specialist grocers, gift and craft shops, cafés, tea shops, restaurants, cake shops, sweet shops and car boot sales. Craft fairs and selling parties at home are also possible outlets. You can also sell on a stall at the garden gate.

Advertising and publicity

If you are selling direct to the public, advertise your preserves in the classified section of a local paper. If you are selling mainly through shops, your advertising should be directed at shop owners, so advertise in trade magazines directed at retailers or write to and visit local shops which are likely to be interested in your wares.

If you are selling preserves as a sideline to selling plants or home-grown fruit and vegetables, tell your customers that you are now selling preserves as well.

How busy? If you sell only at craft fairs and car boot sales, you are your own master and will only have to make enough stock for one sale or fair at a time.

If your products are successful, you can expect to be pressured into keeping up a constant supply, which will keep you very busy. You may prefer to keep the business seasonal and make products only when you have a glut of something. In addition to growing the herbs, fruit or vegetables and turning them into preserves you will be kept busy in other ways: getting labels designed and printed (perhaps even writing them out by hand), bottling, storing and delivering goods.

What to charge It is essential to work out exactly what it has cost you to make each item. Include ingredients, packaging, overheads and time (don't forget costs incurred in the actual growing of the produce). Don't price your goods above up-market, mass-produced, beautifully packaged products of a similar kind. The fact that it almost certainly costs you more to produce your preserves, since they have reached the stage of mass production, makes no difference. You must price competitively. Remember, the more successful you become, the more you will be competing with the big boys.

5
USEFUL
INFORMATION

Where
to sell

The recent interest in fresh, organically grown food has made it much easier for the small supplier to sell his produce and there are various possible outlets. Farm shops, for example, are often happy to take small quantities of locally grown produce, or you can sell from your garden gate or rent a market stall in a local market town. Alternatively you can sell through a local co-operative, or a wholesale distributor, though you would probably have to grow a large quantity to make it worth their while.

Flowers can be sold through local flower shops, at the garden gate, direct to restaurants or contacts can be made for weddings, christenings and funerals through local clubs or the local church. Dried and pressed flowers and related products can be sold at craft fairs, home parties and to gift shops, interior designers or even by mail order. With all craft work it is a good idea to make a prototype in order to test the market.

Co-operatives and distributors

Co-operative to supermarkets
This applies to people growing food crops, including herbs, and it does take the responsibility of advertising, selling and delivering off your shoulders. If you join a co-operative you will have to abide by the rules. Ninety per cent of what you produce may have to be sold through them. This means you will only have enough left for family eating, none for local grocers, health food stores, etc.

You will also be selling at lower prices than if you were retailing the vegetables from your own gate or farm shop.

Co-operatives and distributors can be found through the local Farmers' Union or through farming and horticultural trade journals. If you cannot find the information you want in the pages of the magazine, the editorial staff should be able to help.

Distributors
If you can sell your food crops to a large or a small distributor, again the onus of selling and advertising is taken from you. You will be selling at wholesale prices, but the produce will be collected and you will not have the problem of transport. You will be freer to decide how much you want to sell through the distributor and how much through local outlets.

Other outlets

Independent shops
Health food shops, small greengrocers and farm shops, flower shops and gift shops may be prepared to take small quantities of your freshly picked produce or homemade items. You can arrange prices on an ad hoc basis, but you will have to deliver.

One drawback in selling produce or craft work to shops is that they have to add a mark up to your price to cover their overheads. This may make your product prohibitively expensive for the customer, and you may have to sell to the shop at a discount. On the plus side, if you can find a shop willing to stock your work, it is a way of getting the public to see it.

Some craft shops operate on the principle of dividing the space into a complex of small 'booths', each showing the work of a different craftsperson. If your work is accepted, you might be asked to help in the shop occasionally. If you are not there yourself, you can leave your card for customers to pick up.

Your own shop
This can be a satisfactory way of selling if you know there is a market for your goods. However, it is a major undertaking, and you will need professional advice, a business plan and projected budget and cash flow. You will need a fair amount of capital since you need to rent premises, buy fittings, build up stock, employ help in the shop, pay the bills and so on.

When you see the lease, make sure that there are no restrictions on the sort of business you can run there. Get your solicitor to peruse the lease closely for possible snags. Check that there is no restriction on your transferring the lease to a third party so that you, rather than the landlord, would benefit from selling it.

Choose a shop in a street where likely buyers will see it – preferably next to other similar shops.

Your own farm shop or selling from the garden gate

Depending on how much traffic passes your way, whether it is easy to park, and whether the kind of people passing want to buy produce, you may be able to do quite a good trade selling from the gate or from a farm shop on your premises.

If you want to run a farm shop you will need someone to man it. The fact that you sell a whole range of produce should attract long-term customers.

If you have only a few beans or courgettes to sell, or cut flowers, you could leave a price list and a money box by the gate and let customers help themselves. You will probably not require planning permission (see page 163) but check with your local authority planning office.

Roadside

You may be able to set up a small van or stall for cut flowers, fruit or vegetables in a lay-by. You should first check that the pitch hasn't already been taken by a competitor. You will also have to get planning permission from the local authority planning office. You will have to have a fair amount of produce to make it worthwhile as the stall will have to be manned.

Market stall

A stall in the local market may be a good way to sell your goods, if you have enough. Popular markets sometimes have a long waiting list for a stall, and stalls can be expensive. You may be able to get planning permission to set up a stall in a particular street in town on a particular day.

The Women's Institute run excellent market stalls of home-grown fruit and vegetables, plants and preserves. These markets operate as a separate company, WI Markets, and anyone can sell through them, provided they pay the nominal few pence fee to become a shareholder and are willing to help occasionally on the stall.

Craft markets and fairs

Small local craft markets and fairs are an 'occasional' way of selling which can be useful in terms of sales and meeting possible future customers and other people in the same business with whom you can swap experiences and advice. Make sure you choose the right fair for what you do, and don't waste time and money going to fairs which are unlikely to bring a good response. Some people go to nine or ten fairs a year, others may only attend one or two. There seems to be no question that they are a good way of selling when you are first starting out.

Large national fairs are expensive to attend: stalls are usually costly to rent and you may have to drive some distance to reach them. They usually last several days so you will have to find somewhere to stay overnight unless you have a camper or trailer or are prepared to sleep in a tent. Nevertheless, if a fair is widely publicised it may be worth attending. You might be able to share a stall with a friend or acquaintance selling similar or complementary goods. This will halve the cost and double the interest to the customer.

Car boot sales
These can be good but must be carefully picked. Bric a brac sales will probably be fine for dried or pressed flower pictures and so on but you are unlikely to sell plants with any success unless there is a special plant section.

Plant sales
Plant sales may be held by plant societies, horticultural organisations or colleges. The advantage of plant sales is that you will meet other growers and build up your contacts. (See also Clubs and Societies below).

Clubs and Societies
If you are a member of a society which has something to do with plants or flowers you will probably be able to sell cuttings or plants or even dried flowers at meetings. Many flower arrangers are keen to add unusual flowers to their gardens for use in arrangements and if you are specialising in a particular variety of plant, other enthusiasts will be happy to buy from or swap with you. You won't make much money this way, because prices are kept pretty reasonable within a club. Societies sometimes hold plant sales, which are usually well attended.

Craft societies may hold sales or be able to put you in touch with possible clients.

Home selling parties
A selling party is when a private individual sells something in her own house, or asks other people to sell merchandise from her home. Friends, acquaintances and interested people are then invited to come and inspect the goods and buy if they wish.

If members of the public attend, there are strict rules on how prices are displayed, on 'special' offers, on the condition of the goods and how they are described. But if you hold a party for invited friends only then these rules do not apply. This can be a congenial way of selling homemade things, particularly at Christmas time.

Selling from home
This can be a good way to start when setting up in business. You can be at home one day a week to customers, provided you have a garage or stable or some sort of outhouse to sell from. Local advertising will be necessary but should not be expensive – and anyway you don't want to attract too many people until you have found your feet. See also page 163.

Mail order
The crucial thing here is to advertise in the right places so that potential customers will read the ad. Advertising costs money and so does postage, so don't embark on a business like this until you are ready.

Word of mouth
Sell to friends and neighbours who will then spread the word. This is a good way to start if you enjoy what you are doing but don't want to be committed to a continuous backlog of orders.

Advertising
and publicity

It doesn't matter what you undertake to sell, some form of advertising is going to be essential. Even if you sell jams from your home, you will 'advertise' by word of mouth among friends. Serious advertising in national magazines and newspapers can be a hefty expense so it is important that it should be in the right place at the right time. This isn't always easy to gauge and you may find you make a few mistakes before getting it right. Distributing leaflets is an alternative to advertising in the classified section of a local newspaper.

Generally speaking, it's best to start with minimal advertising until you can size up the response and know how well you can cope with it. The more specialist your product, the more careful you should be about *where* you advertise. If you make a speciality of pressing flowers from bridal bouquets, you will obviously get the best reaction if you advertise in a magazine mostly read by brides-to-be (or their mothers). If your products are food items such as preserves, the classified section of a local paper might be a good place to advertise, or possibly in a national magazine on food.

Word your advertisement or leaflet carefully and make sure readers understand what you are offering. Make the advertisement enticing and stress what is special about your produce or goods. Include details on how to get in touch with you, and at what times you can be contacted if you are not available all the time. If you are out a great deal and rely on telephone replies, install an answering machine so you don't lose important calls.

The local press
A small two-line advertisement in the local paper may bring

people to your street or market stall, or to your doorstep, or bring in telephone orders.

Specialist and national magazines

Magazines will be a good advertising vehicle if you are selling large quantities of herbs and other plants through the post. They are also good for advertising items suitable for gifts just before Christmas. You may have to reserve space a few weeks in advance of publication, so plan ahead.

Leaflets

Informative leaflets which have your name and phone number prominently displayed can be distributed in local shops or car parks, handed out to shoppers, or popped through letter boxes in likely areas.

Roadside signs

These are essential if you want to catch passing trade. You may have to get permission for one of these from the local authority if you are using a roadside verge to display your sign. Make sure the sign is easily legible, large enough to attract attention and gets its message across quickly to someone in a moving car. Have at least two notices made so that they can be seen from each direction. As with an advertisement, make the notice enticing and stress what is special about your produce.

Your own catalogue

Catalogues are not only for business selling by mail order but also an important means of advertising. They should not be too expensive to produce but should be factually correct and easy to read (if the print is too small, this will put people off). Make sure your address is prominently displayed. See page 71 for examples of catalogue wording.

Direct mailing

If you have compiled an address list of previous customers and likely future customers, it may be useful to send them information of your latest products, special Christmas lines, dates and venues of forthcoming craft fairs and home selling parties and names of new stockists of your wares, in addition to your catalogue (if you have one). A large direct mail operation will involve postage and packing costs, so consider carefully who to mail. Be selective and make sure you are offering the right thing to the right person.

Your business card

A business card is invaluable. It will persuade suppliers that you are a serious business, and it can always be handed to an interested party. If you are selling through a shop, restaurant or hotel, ask for permission to leave a small stack of business cards on the premises so that customers can pick one up and contact you personally for special orders.

If you have a business card (and headed note paper) you can buy materials at trade prices from wholesale suppliers and manufacturers, provided you buy in quantity.

Keep the card simple. A well-thought-out and well-designed card will be more appealing and get better results than a carelessly executed one.

Free publicity

This is worth its weight in gold. An editorial feature in a newspaper or magazine should generate a far greater response than an advertisement, and a couple of minutes' interview on a local radio station is more valuable than an expensive advertising slot.

The local press and radio are always looking for interesting things to tell their readers or listeners about, and provided you can persuade them you are doing something a little unusual or timely, they may send someone round to interview you about your business. You can introduce yourself by sending a press release (see below).

When approaching the media, try to find out the name of the journalist who is responsible for editing or writing the relevant section and approach her/him direct. This is usually more productive than writing to The Editor.

Writing a press release

Information on a press release should be succinct and informative. Use one sheet of paper only and head it 'Press Release'. State what you do and indicate what's different or particularly interesting about your service or product. Make sure your address and telephone number are prominent and include a photograph showing an example of your work or goods.

The legal
side

Depending on your type of business, there may be legal requirements governing how you can operate. Don't be put off by these – they exist to protect you and your customers. You will have no problems as long as you are aware of any regulations before you begin trading and seek advice from the relevant authority.

Weights and measures If you are selling fresh fruit and vegetables you will have to comply with weights and measures regulations. Take advice from the local Weights and Measures Inspector. Contact your local Shops Act Inspector who will be able to provide details of bylaws on opening hours, Sunday trading and pavement displays etc.

Where jams and preserves are concerned there may be several regulations as to the size of the jar you are allowed to use, the sugar content and so on (see page 149). There may also be regulations about what you put on the label. Get advice on this before launching into business.

Refreshments If you are offering teas, lunches, ices or any other form of food or drink from your own premises, you will have to comply with the Food Acts and the regulations attached to them. You will have to put up a board with prices near the entrance to the eating area, or if self-service, on the counter. You must also acquaint yourself with the food regulations which include such things as keeping food not less than 45cm (18in) from the ground, having clean food wrappers, providing lavatory facilities and an adequate supply of clean water, wash hand basins, soap and so on, and making sure that you and any staff wear clean and washable over-clothing. As you can see, it is essential to get advice from the Department of Environmental Health before you start.

Food legislation

The moment you make food for sale you become liable to all the regulations relating to food and the first thing you should do is register with the Department of Environmental Health. The Health Inspector will want to inspect your kitchen to see that it conforms with the food hygiene regulations. Inspectors are usually helpful and willing to advise on the health and hygiene aspects of a proposed business. The food regulations contain general requirements for the cleanliness of premises used to prepare food for sale, the hygienic handling of that food and the cleanliness of the people involved in its preparation. Some authorities publish their own detailed guidelines.

The premises where the food is handled must be well ventilated and free from dirt, germs, insects, vermin or bad smells. The floors, walls and ceilings must be easy to clean. There should be a double sink unit for washing food and one for washing equipment.

If you have assistants, you will need sanitary and washing facilities, first aid kits and clothing lockers. But that is the time to consider moving to an industrial unit.

Trading from home

Read the lease on your premises before selling from them. There may be a restrictive covenant which will prevent you from carrying on a trade in premises let to you for domestic purposes. It is unlikely that anyone would notice or object to your selling a few vegetables or bunches of flowers but it is better to be forewarned and you might be able to get your landlord's agreement to the selling of a small surplus.

Check with your mortgage company that there is no restriction to selling from your own premises.

You may need planning permission from the local authority planning office. There are no hard and fast rules about this, but if the business attracts vehicles or customers who disturb neighbours or if it involves activities unusual in a residential area (i.e. lorries and vans starting up at night or loud machinery) you might not be allowed to work from your home. Similarly if your business is going to change the use of the home, if it was no longer used substantially as a private residence, for instance, you would need permission from the council's planning department.

If you are selling from your home, the law requires you to display your name and address somewhere visible at your place of work. You will need permission from the local authority if you want to do this outside your premises.

It would be wise to go through your business plans with a solicitor to make sure you are not contravening regulations you might not be aware of.

If what you are doing creates a domestic hazard (if you use a lot of glues, paint thinners or other flammable materials) you might be wise to move into the garage or find a small industrial unit.

Signs

If you want to put a large notice up at the roadside, advertising your business, you may have to get planning permission from the local authority.

Insurance

All small businesses need insurance. Check with your insurance company whether you are insured for working from home. Discuss with them what cover you need. The main kinds are: insurance of premises, insurance of contents, insurance of stock. These may extend to 'consequential loss' which means that if your mailing address list were to be destroyed, for instance, although of no value in itself, the insurance company would recognise its value to your business.

Then there is employer's liability if you employ people on your premises, and public liability in case you cause injury to a member of the public in the course of business. You might also like to insure against prosecution under Acts of Parliament which relate to your business (e.g. those covering unfair dismissal) and insurance against losing your driving licence. Depending on the size of your business, you may need life insurance and insurance against accident or sickness. Insurance packages are available for small businesses which can make the paperwork simpler.

Check that your motor insurance covers business/ professional use.

The business side

When a hobby becomes a business you need to plan ahead. Of course you won't need to worry about forward planning or cash flow problems if you are selling a few plants or vegetables from the garden, a bunch or two of dried flowers at a car boot sale or making up the odd bouquet for friends. However, it is important to stress the difference in just about every respect between part time, small scale, almost 'accidental' selling and a proper money-making business.

In Britain there are various Government-sponsored schemes organised through local offices of The Training Agency, to help people set up in a small way in business. Some schemes sponsor business training courses, others offer a basic weekly wage for the first year of trading. Ask at your local Job Centre for details or write to Head Office, Moorfoot, Sheffield S1 4PQ, for the address of your nearest regional office.

Finances

If you've had a toe in the water and decide you want to go into business in a more serious way, you will need some capital, if only to buy enough raw materials to get started. You should allow yourself at least three months working capital. If you are opening a shop or need a new greenhouse or have to find a small industrial unit to work in, then you will need more.

You might be lucky enough to have an obliging friend who will lend the money. If so, do it through a solicitor and get a contract drawn up so there are no future misunderstandings. Whether you are approaching a business partner or the bank the first thing you need to do is to produce a convincing business and cash flow plan to show that you are experienced, competent and determined to succeed.

Work out exactly what you need as capital investment to start the business, and how much you need to run it for, say, six months to a year. You must include every smallest item and work out the cost of each with great care. You can lose an awful lot in postage, for example, if you have miscalculated on every parcel, even if it is by only a small amount. Don't forget to allow yourself a wage, and repayments with interest to the bank.

There is bound to be an enlightened bank manager or perhaps a building society or business enterprise scheme manager in the area so don't be disheartened if you have to search around before you find him. It may well not be your own bank manager, who has known you for years and should have faith in your abilities. If your own bank is not particularly cooperative, shop around until you find one that is.

It certainly helps when borrowing if you have a history of successes, however modest, in a similar business. Your first ventures into selling should always be recorded so that you can produce the figures when applying for a capital sum. What the bank manager will want to know is how much of your own money you can invest in the business, your projected cash flow and whether you already have a market.

Remember that it can be as unsatisfactory to borrow too little money (so you start off without quite the right equipment or can't pay for advertising) as it is to borrow too much (so that you are crippled by the interest payable).

Many people who have failed in business were perfectly skilled and meticulous about their work but failed to recognise the importance of a disciplined day or of doing the bookwork or of luring in the customers. You must get the balance right and do all parts of the job well. If that means getting someone else in to do the things you are not so good at, well and good. Make allowances for the possibility of employing someone in your projected costs.

Questions your bank manager will want answered
Be prepared with the answers when you go to see him.

1 Is the project commercially viable and have you already lined up any potential customers/outlets?

2 Have you had experience in a similar business already?

3 Have you any money to put into the business yourself?

4 Have you security to set against the loan?

5 Have you a guarantor for the money?

6 Have you all the skills required for the business (including business skills)?

7 Have you fully researched suppliers and prices of materials and equipment?

8 Have you worked out a budget for the first six months?

Checklist of costs

This list is a general one. Exclude any items which are not relevant and add anything necessary for your own project (for instance you might need a humidifier for drying flowers or a wheel hoe for weeding the vegetable patch).

- Premises, including running costs
- Raw materials
- Tools and equipment, their maintenance and running costs
- Vehicles and their running costs
- Telephone
- Stationery
- Postage and packing
- Insurance of premises, equipment or products; liability insurance
- Advertising
- Book keeper
- Accountant
- Projected income tax
- Employees
- Your time
- If borrowing money, your monthly repayments including interest (allow a margin for a possible rise in interest rates).

Simple accounting

No matter how small your operation, keeping records is important. For one thing you can then justify your expenditure claims to the tax inspector, or prove that you have not earned enough to pay tax.

The first rule is to keep every single receipt, invoice, statement, delivery note and letter in a file, shoe box, box file or on a spike so that you can always verify transactions. Insist on receipts for postage and for every purchase you make on behalf of the business. Fares are not generally receipted so carry a small notebook to jot down business-related expenses such as trade magazines or other small purchases. Tax inspectors are usually fairly sympathetic to beginner businesses who produce this sort of documentation, provided they can see they bear a relationship to the business in question.

A cash book will not only help the tax inspector but will help you to see at a glance how things are balancing out. At its simplest it can be a school exercise book with payments to you on the left hand page and your expenses on the right.

If you reach the stage of making a sizeable profit, you will have to take a more sophisticated attitude towards accounting, but then you can get professional help.

Income tax

If you are simply selling a few plants at a local charity sale, you won't have to worry about income tax. However, it is wise to get in touch with the Inland Revenue pretty early on so that you can find out when you might be liable and how you should prepare for this. No sooner do you start selling through a shop or outside premises than the tax people will be aware of your existence and may end up on your doorstep. At least if you contact them first you know where you stand.

On the whole the tax people are sympathetic towards people setting up on their own and will give advice. If they are on your side from the beginning you are much less likely to have problems later.

If you are a pensioner, the amount you earn may affect your state pension, so you should get advice on this before you make too much money.

If you are unemployed the amount you earn will affect your unemployment benefit. If you work regularly on a part-time basis at your business, you won't be eligible at all, though you might still qualify for a supplementary benefit.

VAT

If your turnover reaches a certain amount (£23,000 a year or £8,000 a quarter, from March 1989) in any one quarter you will have to register for Value Added Tax. This means adding a percentage of your total bill to your invoice and then passing this extra payment on to H.M. Customs and Excise. It is fiddly and time consuming and it is important to apply the rules correctly at all times.

Theoretically it should be some time before you could

hope or wish to be earning so much money that you have to register for VAT. But you might become eligible before you expect to if you buy expensive stock or materials, because the levy is on the total sales or 'output' and not just on the profit. For instance, most garden planners buy plants and other materials (such as paving slabs and compost) for their clients, because that's the easiest way to do things. But the money spent is still counted, for VAT purposes, as turnover. Some people therefore get the client to pay for supplies direct to avoid this. Many small businesses prefer to keep their turnover just under the VAT threshold (by monitoring the jobs they take on very carefully and not receiving large sums of money in any one quarter but staggering their invoices) to save the extra paperwork involved.

Keeping up with book work on a day-to-day basis is important in order not to build up such a backlog that you can't cope with it.

Employing people

If you have got so far with your business that you need extra help, get advice as to the employment laws. It is easier and cheaper to employ part time, self-employed labour than to take on full time employees with all that that entails, e.g. holiday pay, sick pay, pension schemes, notice required, incentive rates, national insurance deductions and so on. Check how many hours a week count as 'part time' (less than 16 in the U.K.). Beyond that you may find yourself caught up in complicated provisions about maternity leave, redundancy and so on and will have to provide employees with rest facilities, lavatories etc.

Check with the Department of Employment for special schemes. For example you can take on unemployed adults and undertake to train them, and the Department of Employment pays their wage. For casual labour, employing somebody every now and then to press flowers, prick out seedlings or plant bulbs, you can take on an unemployed person, a housewife, a pensioner or a schoolchild on a Saturday job as and when you please.

If you want labour on a more permanent basis, the best policy is to take them on as 'sub contractors' or part time self-employed assistants. Partnerships can work perfectly well, but if one person started the business it is unlikely that anybody else, taken on later, will be quite as committed to it.

In a business where you are providing services directly to a client (such as gardening or garden planning) you will probably have to prove to the tax man that ten per cent or more of the income of a self-employed person working for you comes directly from your clients, even if it comes through you. So your invoice to the client should itemise work done by each sub contractor and they in turn should keep their own receipt books and invoice you formally for their work.

Choose people of the right calibre and with the particular skills you need, not just anybody looking for a job. In a garden planning set-up for instance, try to employ people with different interests so that you have a wide variety of expertise to offer: you might have one person who is good at planning, another who is interested in plants. A few men are useful because 'chaps like doing chaps' things such as strimming and edging and working with machines' as one garden planner put it.

Contributors to this book – in order of appearance

Christopher Parker
Eleanor Hodges Rosehaven Organics,
Gamlingay, Sandy, Beds. (If visiting,
please telephone first: (0767) 50142)
Glyn Onione Dove Cottage Herbs, Penn
House Estate, Penn Street, nr Amersham,
Bucks HP7 0PS
Betty Cole
Tracey Duncombe Herbs and Wild Flowers
Dr Tim Ingram Unusual Plants, Copton Ash,
105 Ashford Road, Faversham, Kent
ME13 8XW
Mrs Rose Vesey
Ed Wolf Indoor Garden Design, Unit 5,
Burmarsh Industrial Estate, Marsden Street,
London NW5
Philip Glynn
Toni Willis

Jude Moraes
Sheila Stedman 40 Clarence Road,
Teddington, Mddx TW11 0BW
Patsy Brown
Beryl Bird c/o 'By George', George Street,
St Albans, Hertfordshire
Janie Phillips Macaroni Farm, East Leach,
nr Cirencester, Glos
Josey Read
Joy Hepworth
Susan Ganney Four Seasons Flowers,
14 Coberley Close, Downhead Park,
Milton Keynes MK15 9BJ
Wendy Gunn Pentwyn Cottage, Bacton,
Hertfordshire
Sue Gillies
WI Markets NFWI Markets Department,
39 Eccleston Street, London SW1W 9NT

Useful Addresses

ADAS (Agricultural Development and
Advisory Service) Head Office: 0223 462762.
Branches throughout Britain
Alpine Garden Society Secretary: Michael
Upwood, Lye End Link, St John's, Woking,
Surrey GU21 1SW. 0483 69327
David Anderson & Co (Horticultural
Consultants), Karrelbrook House,
118 Northgate Street, Bury
St Edmunds IP33 1HQ. 0284 701577
The Botanical Society of the British Isles
c/o The Department of Botany, British Museum
(Nat. Hist), Cromwell Road, London SW7 5BD
The Cottage Garden Society 15 Faenol Avenue,
Abergele, Clwyd, Wales. Membership Secretary:
Mrs K Torduff, 5 Nixon Close, Thornhill,
Dewsbury, W Yorks, WF12 0JA
The Crafts Council 1 Oxendon Street,
London SW1
Chartered Association of Certified
Accountants 29 Lincoln's Inn Fields,
London WC2
The Chartered Society of Designers
Bedford Square, London WC1
The Design Council 26 Haymarket,
London SW1
Enterprise Agencies, Development Boards
and Small Firms Service, telephone Freephone
Enterprise and ask for local office

FSPA (Farm Shop and Pick Your Own
Association) National Farmers Union,
Agriculture House, 25–31 Knightsbridge,
London SW1X 7ND. 01–235 5077
Fauna and Flora Preservation Society
Zoological Gardens, Regent's Park, London
NW1
Food From Britain Market Towers,
1 Nine Elms Lane, London SW8 5NQ
The Hardy Plant Society 10 St Barnabas
Road, Emmer Green, Reading, Berks
Henry Doubleday Research Association
and National Centre for Organic Gardening,
Ryton-on-Dunsmore, Coventry CV8 3LG
The Herb Society 77 Great Peter Street,
London SW1
The Law Society 113 Chancery Lane,
London WC2A 1PL
Ministry of Agriculture, Fisheries and Food
Whitehall Place, London SW1
The Mushroom Growers Association
01–235 5077/0732
NCCPG (National Council for Conservation of
Plants and Gardens) (groups throughout
Britain), c/o RHS Wisley, Woking, Surrey
National Association of Flower Arrangement
Societies of Great Britain 21A Denbigh Street,
London SW1V 2HF

National Vegetable Research Station
Wellesbourne, Warwick, CV35 9EF
National Vegetable Society
56 Waun-y-groes Avenue, Rhiwbina, Cardiff
Nature Conservancy Council
Northminster House, Peterborough, Northants
Northern Horticultural Society Harlow Car
Gardens, Harrogate, Yorks HG3 1QB
Royal Horticultural Society Vincent Square,
London SW1P 2PE
The Soil Association 86 Coleston Street, Bristol,
BS1 5BB
Women's Institute Markets (WI Markets),
Voluntary County Market Organiser,
c/o WI County Office (telephone book) or
NFWI Markets Adviser, 39 Eccleston Street,
London SW1W 9NT

Mail order suppliers of seeds

(Send SAE for lists and catalogues)

British Seed Houses Ltd Bewsey
Industrial Estate, Pitt Street, Warrington,
Cheshire WA5 5LE
D T Brown & Co Ltd Station Road,
Poulten-Le-Fylde, Blackpool FY6 7HX
Chiltern Seeds Bartree, Stile,
Ulverston, Cumbria
Dobies Broomhill Way, Torquay, Devon
TQ2 7QW
Emorsgate Seeds Emorsgate,
Terrington Street, Clement, Norfolk
Mr Fothergill's Seeds Gazely Road,
Kentford, Newmarket, Suffolk
S E Marshall & Co Ltd Regal Road,
Wisbech, Cambs PE13 2RT
Samuel Dobie & Son Llangollen, Clwyd, Wales
Sutton's Seeds Torquay, Devon
Tradescant Trust St Mary's Church,
Lambeth, London SE1
Thompson & Morgan London Road, Ipswich,
Suffolk IP2 0BA
Unwin's Seeds Ltd Histon, Cambs CB4 4LE

Mail order suppliers of plants

Burncoose and South Down Nurseries
Gwennap, Redruth, Cornwall TR16 6BJ
Churchill's Garden Nursery Exeter Road,
Chudleigh, Devon TQ13 0DD
Highfield Nurseries
Whitminster, Glos GL2 7PL
Hilliers Nurseries (Winchester) Ltd
Ampfield House, Ampfield, nr Romsey,
Hants SO5 9PA
Hollington Nurseries Woolton Hill,
Newbury, Berks RG15 9XT
Mallorn Gardens Lanner Hill,
Redruth, Cornwall TR16 6DA
Rosemoor Garden Trust Torrington,
Devon EX2 7JY

Organic suppliers

Agriframes Charlwoods Road,
East Grinstead, West Sussex RH19 2HG
(bird netting and fruit cages)
Cowpact Ltd Hokington, Leighton Buzzard,
Bedfordshire LU7 0DN (animal manures)
Organic Concentrates Ltd 3 Broadway Court,
Chesham, Bucks HP5 1EN
Maxicrop Ltd 21 London Road,
Great Shelford, Cambridge CB2 5DF
LBS Polythene Ltd Cottontree, Colne,
Lanes BB8 7BW (Poly tunnels and sheeting)

Courses

City and Guilds (Section 11) 46 Britannia
Street, London WC1X 9RG has over 100 centres
round the country where you can study
practically any aspect of gardening and
acquire a certificate
Denman College Marcham, Abingdon,
Oxon OX13 6NW (owned by the NFWI) runs
courses for men or women who produce for or
help in a WI market with practical
demonstrations and sessions on all aspects of
marketing. Also courses on various crafts using
flowers.
Otley College Otley, Ipswich IP6 9EY
(garden centre management, floristry,
horticulture, countryside conservation)
West Dean College West Dean, Chichester,
West Sussex, PO18 0QZ

Further reading

General

'Practical Guide' series of leaflets on vegetable growing (National Vegetable Research Station)

Henry Doubleday Research Association leaflets (various)

Organic Gardening by Lawrence D Hills (Penguin)

Vegetables Naturally by Jim Hay (Century 1985)

The Allotment Book by Geoff Hamilton, Rob Bullock and Gillie Gould (Optima 1988)

Successful Organic Gardening by Geoff Hamilton (Dorling Kindersley 1987)

Vegetables from Small Gardens by Joy Larkcom (Faber 1976)

Worm Compost by Jack Temple (Soil Association)

Plants Plus (propagation) by George Seddon and Andrew Bicknell (Collins 1987)

The Royal Horticultural Society Encyclopaedia of Plants and Flowers by Christopher Brickell (Dorling Kindersley 1989)

Readers Digest Encyclopaedia of Garden Plants and Flowers (1978)

The Plant Finder compiled by Chris Philip (Headmain/Hardy Plant Society)

Wild Flowers of Britain by Roger Phillips (Pan 1977)

Herb Gardening by Claire Loewenfeld (Faber 1964)

The Wild Garden by Violet Stevenson (Windward 1985)

The Complete Book of Pressed Flowers by Penny Black (Dorling Kindersley 1988)

Pot Pourris and Other Fragrant Delights by Jacqueline Heriteau (Penguin 1988)

The Complete Book of Dried Flowers by Malcolm Hillier and Colin Hilton (Dorling Kindersley 1987)

Flowers by Malcolm Hillier (Dorling Kindersley 1988)

Ikebana by Stella Coe (Octopus 1984)

Success with Houseplants (Readers Digest 1979)

Business books

Working for Yourself by Godfrey Golzen (Kogan Page revised 1988)

The Home Earner by Christine Brady (Corgi 1987)

Home Cooking for Money by Judy Ridgway (Piatkus 1983)

Directory of Enterprise Agencies (Business in the Community)

The Freelance Alternative by Marianne Gray (Piatkus 1987)

Croner's Reference Book for The Self Employed and Smaller Business (Croner Publications Ltd, Croner House, London Road, Kingston Upon Thames, Surrey KT2 6SR)

Daily Telegraph Guide to Effective Advertising for the Small Business by Harry Carter (Kogan Page 1986)

Index